25 Best

NEW YORK CITY

Contents

KEY TO SYMBOLS

➕ Map reference to the accompanying pull-out map

✉ Address

☎ Telephone number

⏰ Opening/closing times

🍴 Restaurant or café

Ⓜ Nearest subway (Metro) station

🚌 Nearest bus route

🚇 Nearest rail station

🚢 Nearest riverboat or ferry stop

♿ Facilities for visitors with disabilities

🅱 Tourist information

❓ Other practical information

🖼 Admission charges: Expensive (over $12), Moderate ($5–$12) and Inexpensive (under $5)

▷ Further information

Introducing New York

"New York is an island off the coast of Europe." There's a lot of truth in this witticism, and it's no wonder this is the city most overseas visitors choose first. The qualities that weld New Yorkers to the city also mark them out as different to heartland America.

Residents of Manhattan value directness, diversity and creativity; they live at a ridiculous pace; they work all hours (they have to, to pay the rent); they walk—fast—everywhere; they fail to keep their opinions to themselves; they have street smarts; they are capital L Liberal. Of the so-called Blue States—those dominated by Democrats—New York is the bluest of them all. The city that actually lived through the 9/11 attack that kicked off an era of paranoia and xenophobia refuses to give in to fear; New Yorkers have all the *chutzpah* they ever did.

In New York, where some hip neighborhood is forever preparing to eclipse the last hot spot, change is the only constant. The crime-ridden, graffiti-scarred mean streets of the late 20th century are but a distant memory. In fact, these days New York is the safest large city in America, according to the FBI Uniform Crime Report. In stark contrast to the gritty days, you'll see strollers (pushchairs) wherever you go, because there is a mini baby-boom in progress. Real estate prices are in the realm of fiction, and a whole lot of regular folks have decamped for Brooklyn, while those who can't afford Brooklyn have gone to Queens. These days parts of Harlem are glamorous and beautiful; the Bronx is next. Staten Island, the fifth borough that most visitors know only for its ferry, is the final frontier.

For many, Manhattan will always be the center of the universe. It's where deals are done, stars are born, legends—and fortunes—are made. Nowhere else in America offers such diversity in fashion, food, design, theater and the arts. The stimulation is addictive, and simply being here is worth a thousand inconveniences. You can take in only so much of the big picture in one visit. So do as New Yorkers do—find a corner of the city and make it your own.

FACTS AND FIGURES

- Visitors in 2014: 56 million (a new record)
- Dollars spent by visitors in 2014: $61 billion
- Hotel rooms by end 2014: 102,000
- Population in 2013: 8.4 million
- Licensed yellow cabs: 13,600
- Feature films shot in New York: more than 250 a year

REAL ESTATE

New York is in the midst of a building boom, with luxury skyscrapers that are among the tallest—and most expensive—in the world. This has put the squeeze on some middle-class New Yorkers. Still, many residents view their homes as not just their castles, but as their portfolio, their retirement plan and their chief financial burden.

BROOKLYN

Once a separate city, the vast borough of Brooklyn across the East River has experienced a migration of disaffected Manhattanites that has changed its character forever. Previously, Brooklyn wasn't trendy; now it's a destination for excellent restaurants, good music venues and great parties in those oh-so-desirable brownstones.

ONE WORLD TRADE CENTER

Nicknamed the Freedom Tower, the new tower in the World Trade Center (▷ 62—63) is officially called One World Trade Center (1WTC). It stands 1,776ft (541m) high—symbolic of the date of U.S. independence—making it the tallest building in America. The stunning observatory opened to the public in spring 2015.

Focus On Architecture

New York is constantly changing, and nowhere is this more apparent than in its architecture. Skyscrapers symbolize the city, but it has many other gems, from ornate art deco office lobbies to the classical columns, carvings and statuary of its Beaux Arts public buildings.

Skyscrapers Past

Although Chicago erected the first skyscraper in 1885, New York embraced the high-rise building style so grandly that it has become the hallmark of the city's skyline. Among the earliest still standing is the 1899 Park Row Building, topped by its distinctive Beaux Arts domes, which at 391ft (119m) held the title of "world's tallest building" for nine years. Other notable early skyscapers include the 1902 Flatiron Building by Daniel Burnham (▷ 68); the 700ft (213m) Metropolitan Life Insurance Tower (1909), modeled after St. Mark's Campanile in Venice; and the neo-Gothic Woolworth Building (1913), at 792ft (241m) the world's tallest until1930.

In Lower Manhattan, skyscrapers grew so thick and fast that the streets of the Financial District started to turn into dark canyons. Zoning laws were passed in 1916, requiring builders to taper the upper storys with "set-backs" to allow light to reach ground level.

By 1930, the race for the top had become a battle of egos, as 40 Wall Street was trumped by the spire of the Chrysler Building (▷ 67), only to lose its title the following year to the Empire State Building (▷ 28–29). It remained the world's tallest building until the World Trade Center towers went up in 1972.

…and Present

From the 1950s onward, art deco elegance gave way to the glass "curtain wall" buildings of the International and Postmodern styles, which are so prominent in Midtown. The

Clockwise from top left: Norman Foster's Hearst Tower; the triangular Flatiron Building; 19th-century Gramercy Park Historic District; interior of the U.S. Custom House,

21st century has seen the addition of such new landmarks to the city skyline as Norman Foster's Hearst Tower (2006), with its gleaming diagonal grid frame. When One World Trade Center (▷ 5) was completed in 2013, New York once again became home to the tallest building in the United States.

Civic and Residential Architecture

But there's much more to New York architecture than these high-rise wonders. Outstanding among its civic buildings are several Beaux Arts beauties, including the U.S. Custom House (1907; ▷ 73), the New York Public Library (1911; ▷ 48–49) and Grand Central Terminal (1913; ▷ 34–35). SoHo's Cast Iron Historic District (▷ 52–53) is lined with elaborate Italianate facades.

Residential architecture is also fascinating in this commercial city, from the brick tenements of the Lower East Side with their zigzagging fire escapes, to the fine brownstone town houses with their high stoops and elaborate doorways lining the leafy streets of Greenwich Village or Brooklyn Heights, to flamboyant luxury apartment buildings like the Ansonia and Dakota overlooking Central Park on the Upper West Side.

Early Relics

Sadly, very little remains in Manhattan from the city's earliest days. Seek out the colonial-era St. Paul's Chapel (▷ 72), the Federal-style warehouses of Schermerhorn Row at South Street Seaport (▷ 72), The Row, a line of Greek Revival houses on the north side of Washington Square (▷ 73), or the delightful 19th-century houses surrounding Gramercy Park, once home to the likes of John Steinbeck (No. 38) and Joseph Pulitzer (No. 17). These survivors are rare gems in a city that is always tearing down the old to make room for the new in its never-ending reach for the stars.

one of New York's finest Beaux Arts buildings; The Row, Washington Square North; the spire of the Chrysler Building; the Woolworth Building's neo-Gothic facade

Top Tips For...

These great suggestions will help you tailor your ideal visit to New York, no matter how you choose to spend your time.

Star Chefs
Jean Georges Vongerichten's restaurant (▷ 146) is the flagship of his ever-growing worldwide empire.
Daniel Boulud at **Café Boulud** will wow you (▷ 143). Be sure to try the madeleines.
Good luck scoring a table at **Per Se** (▷ 148). Thomas Keller has been called the best chef in America. Often.
For fish, nobody matches Eric Ripert at **Le Bernardin** (▷ 142).

Cutting Edge
Trot over to **Jeffrey New York** (▷ 122) to refresh your wardrobe, or, for vintage, **Resurrection** (▷ 124).
Get a taste of the LES at the **Parkside Lounge** (▷ 135).
Have a late supper at **The Spotted Pig** (▷ 149).
Check out the latest show at the **New Museum of Contemporary Art** (▷ 70) or go gallery hopping in **Chelsea** (▷ 66–67).

Partying till Dawn
On Friday and Saturday dance the night away to Latin grooves at **S.O.B.'s** (▷ 137).
Go with the groove at the late-night jazz series at the **Blue Note** (▷ 132) from 12.30am on Friday and Saturday.
Ward off a hangover with a hearty breakfast or some Ukrainian soul food at **Veselka** (▷ 149), open 24 hours.

Big and Beautiful Views
Harbor rooms at the **Ritz-Carlton Battery Park** (▷ 158) include a telescope.
Take in the lake view from Central Park's **Loeb Boathouse** (▷ 147).

Clockwise from top left: Vintage style for sale; view from the Top of the Rock at the Rockefeller Center; FAO Schwarz, a big hit with kids; head to the Blue Note for

Not everyone knows about the **Roof Garden Café and Martini Bar at the Met** (▷ 136). **Top of the Rock** (▷ 51) rivals the **Empire State Building** (▷ 28–29) for views, but the new **One World Observatory** (▷ 63) is the city's highest.

Bringing the Kids
Amaze them with the five-story Ferris wheel inside **Toys R Us**, Times Square (▷ 56–57). You can never go wrong with a good zoo. **Bronx Zoo** (▷ 74) is vast; the one in **Central Park** (▷ 18–19) won't take all day. Take them to **Serendipity 3** (▷ 149) for frozen hot chocolate.
Get tickets for **The New Victory Theater** (▷ 135).
FAO Schwarz is more than a toy store—it's a fantasyland for the child in all of us (▷ 122).

Classic NYC
See the ceiling, covered in toy trucks at the clubby **'21' Club** (▷ 142).
Bergdorf's, Saks and **Bloomingdale's** are classic department stores with different personalities (▷ 120, 125).
The stunning **Chrysler Building** (▷ 67) is New York's favorite skyscraper and an art deco masterpiece.
Walk across the **Brooklyn Bridge** (▷ 66).

Sporting Pursuits
Here in baseball season (April to September)? **Yankee Stadium** (▷ 75) is a must. Or catch the Mets at Citi Field.
Madison Square Garden (▷ 134) has it all: Basketball (the Knicks), boxing, tennis, track and field, hockey, dog shows, and more.
There's a game of something in progress in **Central Park** (▷ 18–19) all summer long.
If it's winter, you can skate at **Wollman Rink**. Shop for stylish outdoor sports gear at **Patagonia** (▷ 124).

late-night jazz; the pedestrian walkway, Brooklyn Bridge; Madison Square Garden; the New Museum of Contemporary Art; Café Boulud, bastion of fine cuisine

Timeline

Pre-1600 New York is populated by Native American groups.

1609 Henry Hudson sails up the Hudson River seeking the Northwest Passage.

1625 "Nieuw Amsterdam" is founded by the Dutch West India Company on the tip of Manhattan Island. The following year the colony's leader purchases the island from the Native Americans for 60 guilders in trade goods.

THE FIGHT FOR INDEPENDENCE

In 1664, Wall Street's wall failed to deter the British, who invaded Manhattan Island and named it New York. The first rumblings of Revolution came in 1765, when Stamp Act protestors rallied in Bowling Green Park. In 1770 the Sons of Liberty fought the British at the Battle of Golden Hill, and in 1776 the American Revolutionary War began and the British chose New York as their headquarters. The Declaration of Independence was read at City Hall Park in July 1776 and the Treaty of Paris ended the war in 1783.

1664 In a bloodless coup, the British take over and rename the island New York.

1776 American Revolutionary War begins.

1783 War ends. Two years later New York becomes the capital of the United States (until 1790).

1789 George Washington is sworn in as first US president at Federal Hall.

1807 Robert Fulton launches the first commercially viable steamboat, revolutionizing shipping.

1827 Slavery in New York is abolished.

1848 Start of the first great waves of immigrants.

1861 New York backs the Union during the Civil War.

1868 The city's first "El" (elevated train) opens.

Inauguration of George Washington on the balcony of Federal Hall in 1789

Immigrants arriving in New York Harbor, 1892

1886 The Statue of Liberty is officially unveiled.

1892 Ellis Island opens.

1904 The first subway opens.

1929 The Great Depression follows the Wall Street Crash.

1933 Prohibition ends after 14 years. Fiorello LaGuardia becomes mayor.

1954 Ellis Island is closed down.

1964 Race riots erupt in Harlem and Brooklyn.

1975 A federal loan saves New York City from bankruptcy.

1990 David Dinkins, New York's first black mayor, takes office.

2001 Terrorists fly two hijacked planes into the twin towers of the World Trade Center, killing an estimated 3,000 people.

2011 The National September 11 Memorial opens at the World Trade Center Site.

2012 The number of visitors to New York City in a single year exceeds 50 million for the first time.

2013 The new tower at One World Trade Center becomes the tallest skyscraper in America.

TENEMENT LIFE

As you make your first explorations in New York, consider how it was for the early immigrants, especially those who were herded through Ellis Island, then crammed into Lower East Side tenements. By the end of the 19th century, the immigrant neighborhoods were dominated by Italians and Eastern European Jews and had become the most densely populated place on earth. Many of these immigrants became garment workers in the ornate cast-iron buildings of SoHo, though many also sewed clothes at their overcrowded homes. Find out more at the Lower East Side Tenement Museum (▷ 69).

Handouts during the Great Depression, following the Wall Street Crash of 1929

The Lower East Side Tenement Museum

Top 25

This section contains the must-see Top 25 sights and experiences in New York. They are listed alphabetically, and numbered so you can locate them on the inside front cover.

TOP 25

American Museum of Natural History

1

HIGHLIGHTS

- Blue whale
- Barosaurus
- Cape York meteorite
- Dinosaur halls
- Journey to the Stars
- Star of India
- Animal dioramas
- Dinosaur embryo
- IMAX theater shows

TIP

- You can observe the entire life cycle of tropical butterflies from October to June at the Butterfly Conservatory.

Of the 36 million items owned by the American Museum of Natural History—the largest such institution in the world—only a small fraction is on show. Don't miss the renowned dinosaur halls and stunning animal dioramas in native habitats.

Star attractions The original museum building opened in 1877, and as it grew its facade sported pink brownstone and granite towers, turrets and a grand Beaux Arts entrance on Central Park West. This opens into a soaring rotunda containing the museum's beloved icon, that of a cast of a Barosaurus rearing up to her full 55ft (17m) to protect her young from an Allosaurus attack. There's far too much to see in one day, with four city blocks and the entire evolution of life on Earth covered. In the

Left: The magnificent rotunda of the American Museum of Natural History is dominated by the skeleton of a Barosaurus; below: The stunning Rose Center for Earth and Space, adjoining the museum, includes the Hayden Planetarium where Space shows take place

adjoining Rose Center for Earth and Space, a giant sphere contains the Big Bang Theater and the Hayden Planetarium, where thrilling space shows are projected on the dome.

More gems The 563-carat Star of India sapphire is part of the Hall of Meteorites, Minerals and Gems, which contains almost $50 million worth of precious stones, plus the Cape York meteorite. Another highlight is the enormous model of a blue whale looming over the Hall of Ocean Life. The museum is best known for its splendid dinosaur halls, where real fossil specimens (rather than models) of an Apatosaurus and the first Tyrannosaurus rex ever exhibited are displayed. Equally impressive are the *tableaux morts* of animals from around the world, set in dioramas of great artistic merit.

THE BASICS

www.amnh.org

➕ C6

✉ Central Park West/79th Street

☎ 212/769-5100

🕐 Daily 10–5.45; closed major public holidays

🍴 Various

🚇 B, C 81st Street-Museum of Natural History

🚌 M7, M10, M11, M79, M86, M104

♿ Good

💲 Expensive

❓ 1-hour tours from 10.15 until 3.15. Rose Center drinks and dancing 2nd or 3rd Friday of month, 9pm–1am. Tel 212/769-5200 for advance reservations for special exhibits and events

HIGHLIGHTS

- Williamsburg
- Brooklyn Heights Promenade
- Bandshell concerts
- The Theater and Rose Cinema at BAM
- Brooklyn Museum of Art

TIP

- New York Fun Tours run Best of Brooklyn Multicultural Ethnic Neighborhood Food Tasting and Culture tours four times a week (www. newyorkfuntours.com).

Brooklyn has it all—one of the largest art museums in the US and some of New York's best restaurants; beaches and a park; a zoo, aquarium and children's museum; hip neighborhoods and avant-garde arts.

Big, bigger, biggest If Brooklyn were still a separate city, it would be the fourth largest in the US. Home to more than 2.5 million people, it is the most populous of New York's boroughs with Russian, Middle Eastern, Italian, West Indian, Hasidic Jewish and Chinese neighborhoods. The Brooklyn Museum of Art, intended by architects McKim, Mead & White to be the biggest museum in the world (it's actually the seventh largest in the US), has collections ranging from pre-Columbian art to 58 Rodin sculptures, plus what many feel are the best

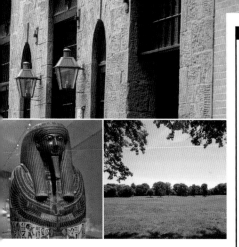

Clockwise from far left: The Gothic arches and cables of the Brooklyn Bridge; gentrified mews houses in the desirable residential area of Brooklyn Heights; Prospect Park; the excellent Brooklyn Museum of Art includes an outstanding Egyptian collection

THE BASICS

Brooklyn Heights
➕ H22
🚇 2, 3 Clark Street
Brooklyn Museum of Art
www.brooklynmuseum.org
➕ See map ▷ 110
✉ 200 Eastern Parkway
☎ 718/638-5000
🕐 Wed, Fri–Sun 11–6, Thu 11–10
🚇 2, 3, Eastern Parkway-Brooklyn Museum
♿ Moderate
Prospect Park
➕ See map ▷ 110
☎ 311 or 718/965-8999
🚇 2, 3 Grand Army Plaza Station; F 15th Street–Prospect Park
Williamsburg
➕ See map ▷ 111
Brooklyn Flea and Smorgasburg
www.brooklynflea.com
✉ East River State Park, 50 Kent Street
🕐 Smorgasburg: Saturday; Brooklyn Flea: Sunday; check website for details
🚇 L Bedford Avenue
♿ Inexpensive

Egyptian rooms outside Egypt and the British Museum. Steps from the museum's grand entrance is the Botanic Garden. Then, farther south, wander in Prospect Park, where summertime events and the zoo are highlights.

The bridge and beyond Brooklyn Bridge Park is an 85-acre (26ha) greenway reclaimed from derelict piers along the Brooklyn Heights waterfront, featuring jogging paths, water sports, and outdoor festivals. From Brooklyn Heights you can climb stairs to the Brooklyn Bridge pedestrian crossing. Or visit the Promenade for its view of Manhattan. Williamsburg is among the trendiest spots in the city, featuring restaurants, clubs, artisanal foods and crafts, and, in warm weather, the renowned Brooklyn Flea and Smorgasburg food fest at the river's edge.

HIGHLIGHTS

- Delacorte Theater, Shakespeare in the Park
- Summer stage concerts
- Conservatory Water
- Bethesda Fountain
- Wollman Rink in winter
- Heckscher Playground
- Swedish Cottage Marionette Theatre
- Walking in the Ramble

TIPS

- Don't walk alone in isolated areas at night.
- Watch out for bicycles on the roads.

The park is the escape valve for the city. Without it New York would overheat—especially in summer, when the humidity tops 90 percent. Bikers, runners, dog strollers and frisbee players convene here. It's a way of life.

The Greensward Plan In the mid-19th century, when few lived in Manhattan north of 42nd Street, *New York Evening Post* editor William Cullen Bryant campaigned until the city invested $5 million in 843 acres (340ha) of undeveloped land. Responsible for clearing the land was journalist Frederick Law Olmsted, who, with English architect Calvert Vaux, also won the competition to design the park with his "Greensward Plan." Five million cubic tons of dirt were cleared to create this green space.

Clockwise from left: The Pond, at the south end of Central Park; a bronze statue depicting characters in Lewis Carroll's Alice in Wonderland, *just north of the Conservatory Water; Sheep Meadow, a great place to throw frisbees; the tribute to John Lennon in Strawberry Fields*

Fun and games Start at the Dairy Information Center and pick up a map and events list. These show the layout of the park and tell you about the Wildlife Conservation Center (Zoo), the Carousel, the playgrounds, rinks, fountains, statues and Strawberry Fields, where John Lennon is commemorated close to the Dakota Building, where he lived and was shot. But the busy life of the park is not recorded on maps: music making on the Mall; sunbathing in the Sheep Meadow; hanging out at the Heckscher Playground and Great Lawn softball leagues; doing the loop road by bike; sailing toy boats on the Conservatory Water; bird-watching in the Ramble; jogging around the Reservoir; rowing on the Lake beneath the lovely Bow Bridge; fishing at Harlem Meer; or bouldering on the outcrops of Manhattan schist (rock).

THE BASICS

www.centralparknyc.org
➕ D2–D9
☎ 212/310-6600
🕐 Dairy Information Center daily 10–5
🍴 Restaurants, kiosks
🚇 A, B, C, D, 1 59th Street–Columbus Circle; N, Q, R 57th Street–7th Avenue or 5th Avenue–59th Street, F 57th Street; 4, 5, 6 86th Street
🚌 M1, M2, M3, M4, M5, M10. Crosstown M66, M30, M72, M86
♿ Moderate
🎟 Free

HIGHLIGHTS

● Mahayana Buddhist
Temple (✉ 133 Canal
Street 🕐 Daily 8.30–6
💰 Donation)
● Museum of Chinese in
America (✉ 215 Centre
Street ☎ 212/619-4785
🕐 Tue–Wed, Fri–Sun 11–6,
Thu 11–9 💰 Moderate)
● Pearl River Mart (✉ 477
Broadway, ▷ 122)
● Doyers Street
● Columbus Park
(✉ Bayard/Baxter streets)

TIP

● On a warm weekend,
head for Sara Delano
Roosevelt Park, near
Broome and Chrystie
streets, where people air
their songbirds in ornate
cages around the Wah-Mei
Bird Garden.

New York's Chinatown has swallowed
nearly all of Little Italy and has spread over
a great deal of the Lower East Side. Wander
here and you're humbled by the sights and
sounds of a busy Asian community.

Going west Chinese people first came to New
York in the late 19th century, looking to work,
make some money and return home. But, by
1880, some 10,000 men—mostly Cantonese
railroad workers—settled among the Irish and
Italians of the old Five Points area. The Chinese
Exclusion Act (1883) kept the community small
until immigration restrictions were lifted in
1965. While the first arrivals were mostly
Cantonese speakers, most of today's immigrants are Fujianese. New York has two more
Chinatowns: In Flushing (Queens) and Eighth

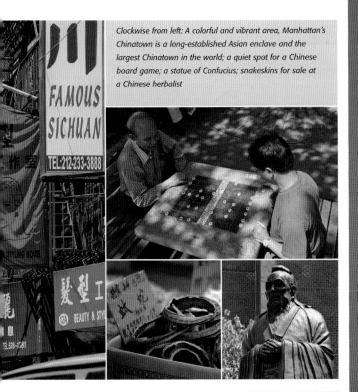

Clockwise from left: A colorful and vibrant area, Manhattan's Chinatown is a long-established Asian enclave and the largest Chinatown in the world; a quiet spot for a Chinese board game; a statue of Confucius; snakeskins for sale at a Chinese herbalist

Avenue, Brooklyn, with thousands of residents. Manhattan's, though, is the world's largest.

A closed world Although you may happily wander its colorful streets, you will never penetrate Chinatown. Many of its denizens never learn English and never leave its environs. Hundreds of factories and restaurants keep them in work; then there are the tea shops, mahjong parlors, herbalists and the highest bank-to-citizen ratio in New York. Catch a glimpse of this vibrant culture at the Mahayana Buddhist Temple, with its 16ft (4.8m) Buddha; in Columbus Park, where residents practice tai chi; at the fish and produce markets on Mott Street; or on tiny Doyers Street, known as "the Bloody Angle" in the early 1900s for the gang warfare that went on there.

THE BASICS

✚ F19–20

✉ Roughly delineated by Worth Street/East Broadway, the Bowery, Grand Street, Centre Street

🍽 Numerous (some close around 10pm)

🚇 6, N, Q, R, J, Z Canal Street; B, D Grand Street

🚌 M22, M103

♿ Poor

❓ For general tours: www.explorechinatown.com

Visitors' Kiosk at Canal and Baxter streets, daily 10–6

5 Cooper Hewitt Smithsonian Design Museum

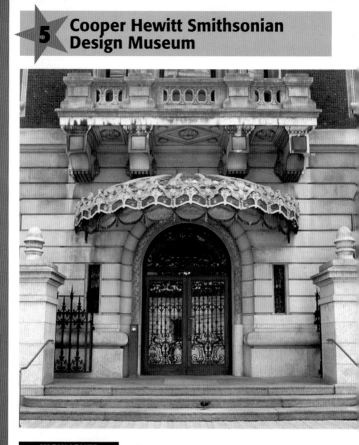

HIGHLIGHTS

- Original 1903 detailing
- HD touch-screen tables
- Immersion Room
- Process Lab
- Garden
- Summer concerts
- Textile collection

TIP

- Love old mansions? The nearby Neue Gallerie (▷ 70) and Jewish Museum (▷ 68) are both housed in wonderful Gilded Age homes.

Having reopened in December 2014 after a three-year, multimillion-dollar renovation, America's sole design museum is now 60 percent larger, thanks to an expansion of the landmark Carnegie Mansion that involved 13 design firms.

Carnegie and Cooper and Hewitt The mansion that contains this superb collection belonged to industrialist Andrew Carnegie, who, in 1903, had asked architects Babb, Cook & Willard for "the most modest, plainest and most roomy house in New York City." This he did not receive (aside from the roominess), since this little chateau was built with modern conveniences galore—air-conditioning and elevators—and a big gated garden. The entire neighborhood came to be known as Carnegie

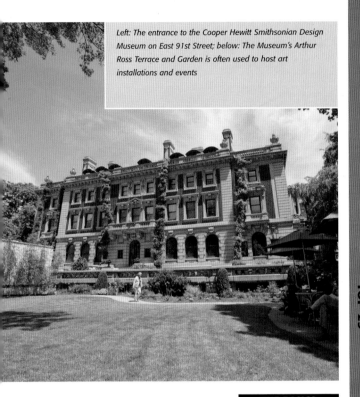

Left: The entrance to the Cooper Hewitt Smithsonian Design Museum on East 91st Street; below: The Museum's Arthur Ross Terrace and Garden is often used to host art installations and events

Hill. Andrew's wife, Louise, lived here until her death in 1946. Twenty years later, the collection of the Hewitt sisters (decorative arts, ceramics, textiles, and more), which had been previously exhibited at the Cooper Union (▷ 24) became a part of the Smithsonian and moved into the mansion.

State of the Art The museum's revamp is designed to make its exhibitions more interactive. In the Immersion Room, you can project textile patterns onto blank walls and then create your own. In the Process Lab you can make your own prototype or see a 3D printer in action. However, these state-of-the-art exhibits have not displaced the Hewitt sisters' core collection and Carnegie's home is still shown to good effect.

THE BASICS

www.cooperhewitt.org

🔂 E4

✉ 2 E 91st Street

☎ 212/849-8400

🕐 Sun–Fri 10–6, Sat 10–9. Closed Thanksgiving, Christmas, New Year's Day

🍴 Café

🚇 4, 5, 6 86th Street

🚌 M1, M2, M3, M4

♿ Good

💲 Expensive

❓ Free tours daily

6 East Village and NoHo

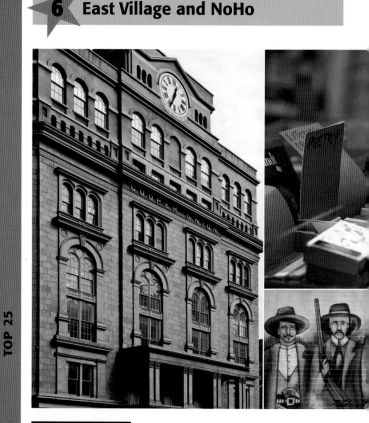

HIGHLIGHTS

● Merchant's House Museum
● Strolling St. Mark's Place
● Diverse array of foods

TIP

● The Strand (▷ 125) on Broadway has 18 miles (29km) of shelves packed with new and used titles. In an area that was once lined with second-hand book-shops, the Strand is one of the few remaining places to find obscure titles.

Once an immigrant neighborhood—and then the rundown bohemia celebrated in the musical *Rent*—the East Village is now prime real estate. Nearby NoHo is quieter and full of historic streets and sites.

Early days What was once Dutch Governor Peter Stuyvesant's farm, or bowery, later became a mostly German enclave. Jews, Poles, and Ukrainians followed. Meanwhile, streets such as Bond and Lafayette in what is today the section called NoHo (North of Houston) were home to New York's mercantile elite, including John Jacob Astor, the country's richest man.

Historic sites Cooper Union, founded by industrialist Peter Cooper and built in 1859, was the spot where Abraham Lincoln gave his

Clockwise from far left: Cooper Union, an East Village landmark; trading on the area's literary associations; the neighborhood's Ukrainian heritage is celebrated at the Ukrainian Museum; architectural detail inside Grace Church; an East Village mural

landmark "Right Makes Might" anti-slavery speech. The city's second-oldest church, St. Mark's-Church-in-the-Bowery, boasts Peter Stuyvesant's grave. On Broadway, Grace Church (▷ 68) was the debut of architect James Renwick, who'd go on to build St. Patrick's Cathedral (▷ 71). The Ukrainian Museum, in the heart of the immigrant neighborhood, features textiles, and beautifully decorated Easter eggs. In NoHo, the Merchant's House Museum is an intact early 19th-century home lived in by the same family for nearly a century.

St. Mark's Place The main thoroughfare of the East Village is St. Mark's. In the 1960s, counter-culture exploded along this street, which included Andy Warhol's Electric Circus. Today it is a mix of shops, restaurants and tattoo parlors.

THE BASICS

➕ F16; east of Broadway and south of 14th Street
🚇 F, M Lower East Side-2nd Avenue; 6 Astor Place

Ukrainian Museum
www.ukrainianmuseum.org
➕ F17
✉ 222 E 6th Street/2nd–3rd avenues
☎ 212/228-0110
🕐 Wed–Sun 11.30–5
♿ Moderate

Merchant's House Museum
www.merchantshouse.org
➕ E17
✉ 29 E 4th Street/Lafayette-Bowery
☎ 212/777-1089
🕐 Thu–Mon 12–5
♿ Poor
♿ Moderate

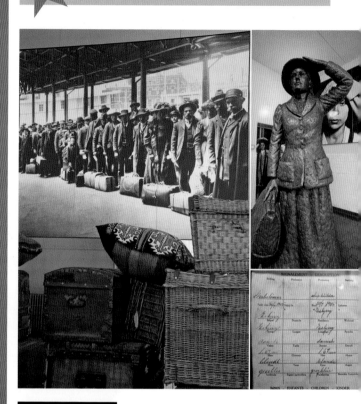

HIGHLIGHTS

● Wall of Honor
● Peopling of America galleries
● The American Flag of Faces™

TIP

● To avoid lines and wait times, try to be on the first ferry to Ellis Island (which also serves the Statue of Liberty). The lines and wait times to board ferries grow exponentially during the day, especially in summer.

Visiting Ellis Island, the gateway to America for millions of immigrants from 1892–1954, is a poignant reminder of the obstacles so many people had to overcome to reach this country.

Half of all America It was the poor immigrants who docked at Ellis Island, since travelers in first-class passage were given permission to disembark straight into Manhattan. Young Annie Moore, aged 15 and the first immigrant to land at Ellis Island, arrived in 1892. She was followed by some 16 million immigrants over the next 40 years, including such future success stories as Irving Berlin and Frank Capra. Unsurprisingly, around one-third of the current population of the United States can trace their roots to an Ellis Island immigrant.

Clockwise from far left: Exhibition documenting the arrival of early immigrants to New York; statue of Annie Moore, the first immigrant to arrive at Ellis Island; the Great Hall; view of Ellis Island from the ferry; the view of Lower Manhattan from Ellis Island; an immigrant's records

Island of Tears The exhibition in the main building conveys the indignities, frustrations and fears of the immigrants. (On arrival, collect your free ticket for the half-hour film, *Island of Hope, Island of Tears*.) A free, 45-minute audio tour accompanies you around the route that new arrivals took, from the Baggage Room, where people had to abandon all they owned, then onward to the Registry Room and through the inspection chambers, where the medical, mental and political status of each immigrant was ascertained. In the museum, the American Family Immigration History Center® gives access to passenger ship records of millions of immigrants. The brilliant new Peopling of America galleries tell of the hardships and struggles of immigrants in the years preceding and post the island's processing station.

THE BASICS

www.nps.gov/elis

⊞ See map ▷ 110

✉ Ellis Island

☎ 212/363–3200

🕐 Daily 9.30–5; extended hours in summer

🍴 Café

Ⓢ 4, 5 Bowling Green, 1 South Ferry, then take ferry

🚌 M5, M20, M15 South Ferry, then take the ferry

🛳 Ferry departs Battery Park South Ferry every 30 min. Ferry information, tel 877/523-9849; www.statuecruises.com

♿ Good

🎟 Museum free; ferry expensive

❓ Audio tours

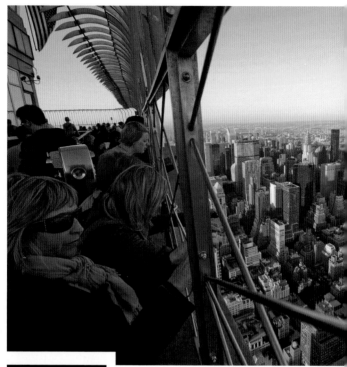

HIGHLIGHTS

● The view at any time of day or night
● The view up from 34th Street
● Observatory Audio Tour
● Marble art-deco lobby

TIPS

● You can avoid the line (though not security check) by printing out advance tickets from the website.
● The colored lights at the summit were introduced in 1976 and are changed to mark different events.

Though she lost her crown as world's tallest building more than four decades ago, the Empire State Building remains New York's most famous skyscraper. Known around the world from movies such as *King Kong*, *An Affair to Remember* and *Sleepless in Seattle*, the 86th-floor Observatory is worth the long lines.

King for 40 years This is the very definition of "skyscraper," and it was the highest in America until the late, lamented World Trade Center was built in the 1970s. Now it has once again been overtaken as the tallest building in New York, this time by One World Trade Center.

Construction began in 1930, not long before the great Wall Street Crash. By the time it was topped out in 1931—construction went at the

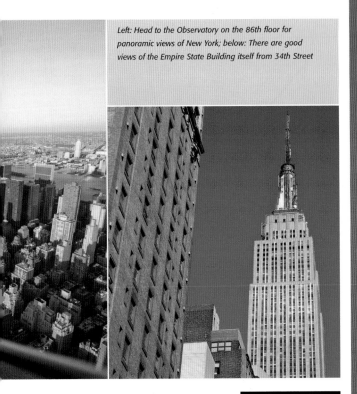

Left: Head to the Observatory on the 86th floor for panoramic views of New York; below: There are good views of the Empire State Building itself from 34th Street

superfast rate of four stories a week—few could afford to rent space, and they called it "the Empty State Building." Only the popularity of its observatories kept the wolves from the door. These viewpoints still attract up to four million visitors each year. The open-air 86th floor Observatory is a highlight.

The facts It is 1,454ft (443m) high, with 103 floors. The frame contains 60,000 tons of steel, 10 million bricks line the building, and there are 6,500 windows. The speediest elevator climbs about 1,000ft (330m) per minute. The fastest runners in the annual Empire State Run-Up climb the 1,860 steps (not open to the public) to the 102nd floor in just over nine minutes. The observation deck on the 102nd floor requires a separate ticket and additional fee.

THE BASICS

www.esbnyc.com
⊞ D13
✉ 350 5th Avenue/ W 34th Street
☎ 212/736-3100
🕐 Daily 8am–2am; last admission 1.15am
🍴 Restaurants
🚇 B, D, F, N, Q, R 34th Street–Herald Square
🚌 M1, M2, M3, M4, M5
🚉 PATH 34th Street– Avenue of the Americas
♿ Good
💲 Expensive

HIGHLIGHTS

- Shopping!
- Empire State Building
- Rockefeller Center
- The Met
- The Guggenheim
- Cooper Hewitt

TIP

- Try to see a parade—St. Patrick's Day Parade, the biggest, is on March 17.

Think shopping in New York, and Fifth Avenue is likely to be your next thought. But there is more here: Museums, hotels and landmark buildings rub shoulders with FAO Schwarz, Saks Fifth Avenue and an Apple Store that never closes.

Tradition and invention Fifth Avenue runs all the way from Washington Square Park up past Central Park and houses some of the most pricey and notable real estate in New York. Walk along the avenue and you'll pass the Flatiron Building (▷ 68), the Empire State Building (▷ 28–29), the New York Public Library (▷ 48–49), Rockefeller Center (▷ 50–51), St. Patrick's Cathedral (▷ 71), the Frick Collection (▷ 32–33), the Metropolitan Museum of Art (▷ 44–45), the Guggenheim

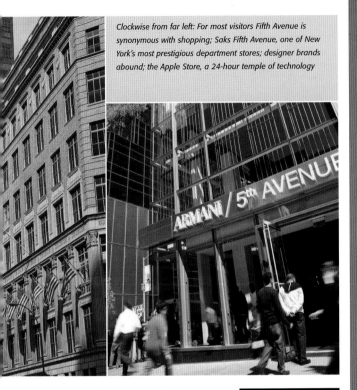

Clockwise from far left: For most visitors Fifth Avenue is synonymous with shopping; Saks Fifth Avenue, one of New York's most prestigious department stores; designer brands abound; the Apple Store, a 24-hour temple of technology

(▷ 38–39), and the Cooper Hewitt Smithsonian Design Museum (▷ 22–23), just a few of the buildings that represent the development of Fifth Avenue.

Shop, shop, shop If you have kids, head for FAO Schwarz toy store (▷ 122). Grown-ups might prefer the jewelry emporia of Tiffany & Co. (57th Street) and Cartier (No. 653), the 24-hour Apple Store (▷ 119) or the department stores. Saks Fifth Avenue (▷ 125) has been here since 1922. Bergdorf Goodman (▷ 120) is at 58th Street, and the fashion mecca Henri Bendel is at 56th, along with Abercrombie & Fitch. If you plan to shop till you drop, two excellent hotels stand opposite each other on Fifth Avenue and 55th Street: The Peninsula New York and the St. Regis (▷ 158).

THE BASICS

➕ E16–E7
✉ From Washington Square to the Harlem River
🚇 4, 5, 6 (various stops), R 5th Avenue–59th Street, E, M 5th Avenue–53rd Street
🚌 M1, M2, M3, M4

HIGHLIGHTS

● *St. Jerome*, El Greco (c.1590–1600)
● *Sir Thomas More*, Holbein (1527)
● *Officer and the Laughing Girl*, Vermeer (c.1657)
● *The Polish Rider*, Rembrandt (c.1655)
● *The Progress of Love*, Fragonard (1771–72)
● *Philip IV of Spain*, Velázquez (1644)

To step inside Henry Clay Frick's magnificent Beaux Arts mansion on Fifth Avenue is half the reason for coming here. Henry Frick bequeathed his riches to the nation as a memorial to himself—that's the kind of guy he was.

The man and the mansion Henry Clay Frick (1849–1919) was chairman of the Carnegie Steel Corp. (US Steel). He was a ruthless strike-breaker and one of the nastiest industrialists of his day. Instead of receiving any comeuppance (though there were assassination attempts), he got to commission Carrère and Hastings to build him one of the last great Beaux Arts mansions on Fifth Avenue and filled it with an exquisite collection of 14th- to 19th-century paintings, porcelain, furniture and bronzes.

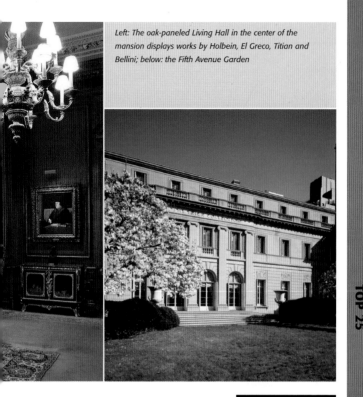

Left: The oak-paneled Living Hall in the center of the mansion displays works by Holbein, El Greco, Titian and Bellini; below: the Fifth Avenue Garden

What Frick bought Some of the 40 rooms are arranged around a particular work or artist, notably the Boucher Room, east of the entrance, and the Fragonard Room, with the *Progress of Love* series. There are British masters (Constable, Gainsborough, Whistler, Turner), Dutch (Vermeer, Rembrandt, Van Eyck, Hals), Italian (Titian, Bellini, Veronese) and Spanish (El Greco, Goya, Velázquez). Interspersed with the paintings are Limoges enamel and Chinese porcelain, Persian carpets and Marie Antoinette's furniture. You can admire a Louis XVI chair before strolling through the central glass-roofed courtyard. The Fifth Avenue Garden is a delight also.

Much of the mansion remains off view to visitors, including the second-floor private apartments and a bowling alley in the basement.

THE BASICS

www.frick.org
✚ E7
✉ 1 E 70th Street
☎ 212/288-0700
🕐 Tue–Sat 10–6, Sun 11–5; closed public holidays
🚇 6 68th Street–Hunter College
🚌 M1, M2, M3, M4
♿ Good
💶 Expensive
❓ Audio tours; for concerts, lectures and docent talks see calendar

HIGHLIGHTS

● Main concourse ceiling
● Oyster Bar
● Chandeliers
● Whispering Gallery
● The clock
● The 75ft (23m) arched windows
● Grand Staircase
● The Dining Concourse (▷ 145)
● The Campbell Apartment cocktail bar

TIP

● After admiring the building, visit the many boutiques, gourmet market, and the annex of the New York Transit Museum.

Don't call it a station. All tracks terminate here, which makes it—yes—a terminal. The Beaux Arts building bustles like nowhere else. As the saying goes—stand here long enough and the entire world passes by.

Heart of the nation "Grand Central Station!" bellowed (erroneously) the 1937 opening of the eponymous NBC radio drama; "Beneath the glitter and swank of Park Avenue… Crossroads of a million private lives!…Heart of the nation's greatest city…" And so it is, and has been since 1871 when the first, undersize version of the station was opened by Commodore Cornelius Vanderbilt, who had bought up all the city's railroads. See him in bronze below Jules-Alexis Coutan's allegorical

Clockwise from far left: The concourse of Grand Central Terminal; statuary by Jules-Alexis Coutan on the main facade; Grand Central subway station; the Campbell Apartment cocktail bar; the four-faced clock; enjoy a platter of oysters in the famous Oyster Bar

statuary on the main facade (south, 42nd Street). The current building dates from 1913 and is another Beaux Arts glory, its design modeled partly on the Paris Opéra by the architectural firm Warren and Wetmore.

Look within Inside, the main concourse soars 12 stories high, with gleaming gold chandeliers and grand marble staircases at either end. Be careful what you say here—the acoustics are amazing. Look up at the ceiling for the stunning sight of 2,500 "stars" in a cerulean sky, with zodiac signs by French artist Paul Helleu. The fame of the four-faced clock atop the information booth is out of proportion to its size. Below ground is a warren of 32 miles (52km) of tracks, tunnels and chambers; in one the famed Oyster Bar resides.

THE BASICS

www.grandcentralterminal.com

🔳 E11

✉ E 42nd Street/Park Avenue

☎ 212/340-2583

🕐 Daily 5.30am–2am

🍴 Restaurant, café/bar, snack bars 🚇 4, 5, 6, 7, S Grand Central–42nd Street

🚌 M1, M2, M3, M4, M42, M101, M102, M103 Grand Central 🚃 Metro North, Grand Central

♿ Good 💲 Free

❓ Municipal Art Society guided tours daily, 12.30pm; tickets (expensive) from the ticket window in the main concourse. Self-guided audio tours (moderate), daily 9–6, from GCT Tour windows on the main concourse

TOP 25

HIGHLIGHTS

- Cafés and jazz clubs
- Washington Square Park
- NYC's narrowest house (75 1/2 Bedford Street)
- Christopher Park
- Halloween Parade
- Jefferson Market Library
- Italian restaurants on Bleecker Street
- Minetta Lane

TIP

- Bleecker Street, one of the main drags through the Village, is lined with one-of-a-kind stores, music bars and great pizza parlors.

The Village (never just "Greenwich") has long been a bohemian mecca, and its picturesque neighborhoods lined with trees and brownstones form a romantic image of Manhattan.

Artists, writers, musicians First settled by the Dutch as Noortwijck, the Village became a refuge in the 18th and early 19th centuries for wealthy New Yorkers escaping epidemics in the city. When the elite moved on, the bohemian invasion began. Edgar Allan Poe moved to West Third Street in 1845. Fellow literary habitués included Mark Twain, O. Henry, Walt Whitman, F. Scott Fitzgerald and Eugene O'Neill. After World War II, artists Jackson Pollock, Mark Rothko and Willem de Kooning also lived here. Bob Dylan made his name in Village music

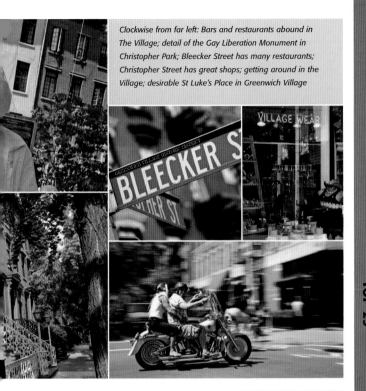

Clockwise from far left: Bars and restaurants abound in The Village; detail of the Gay Liberation Monument in Christopher Park; Bleecker Street has many restaurants; Christopher Street has great shops; getting around in the Village; desirable St Luke's Place in Greenwich Village

VILLAGE WEAR

GREENWICH VILLAGE HISTORIC DISTRICT

BLEECKER S

clubs in the 1960s, while the Blue Note (▷ 132) and Village Vanguard clubs remain hotbeds of jazz today.

Freedom parades When police raided the Stonewall Inn on June 28, 1969, and arrested gay men for illegally buying drinks, they set off the Stonewall Riots—the birth of the Gay Rights movement. The Inn is on Christopher Street, which became the center of New York's gay community. Statues of gay and lesbian couples stand in tiny Christopher Park. The Washington Memorial Arch (▷ 73) towers over Washington Square Park, a lively hangout for university students. As you explore, look out for the ornate Jefferson Market Library (6th Avenue and W 10th Street), the quaint Cherry Lane Theatre on Commerce Street, and tiny Minetta Lane.

THE BASICS

➕ C17–D17
✉ East–west from Broadway to Hudson Street; north–south from 14th Street to Houston Street
🍴 Numerous
🚇 A, B, C, D, E, F 4th Street–Washington Square; 1 Christopher Street–Sheridan Square
🚌 M5
🚉 PATH Christopher Street
♿ Poor

TIP

● Museum admission is pay-what-you-wish on Saturdays 5.45–7.45, but get there early as lines can be long.

Now considered one of his masterpieces, Frank Lloyd Wright's spiral-shaped museum building was originally derided by critics, who compared it to a jello mold.

Museum of architecture This is the great architect's only major New York building. It was commissioned by Solomon R. Guggenheim at the urging of his friend and taste tutor Baroness Hilla von Rebay, though unfortunately, the wealthy metal-mining magnate died 10 years before it was completed in 1959.

The giant white nautilus is certainly arresting, but it's the interior that unleashes the most superlatives. Take the elevator to the top level and snake your way down the museum's spiral ramp to experience the full effects of the building's design. You can study the exhibits (albeit

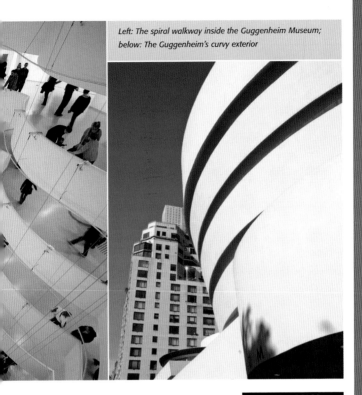

Left: The spiral walkway inside the Guggenheim Museum; below: The Guggenheim's curvy exterior

in reverse order), look over the parapet to the lobby below and finish up where you began.

Museum of art There are some 6,000 pieces in the Guggenheim Foundation's possession. Solomon and his wife Irene Rothschild abandoned collecting old masters when Hilla von Rebay introduced them to Léger, Kandinsky, Chagall, Mondrian, Moholy-Nagy and Gleizes, and they became hooked on the moderns. See early Picassos in the small rotunda and the tower extension. For Impressionists and Postimpressionists, look for the Thannhauser Collection, always on display—unlike the rotated Guggenheim holdings, which are shown in themed exhibitions. The museum continues to acquire works, including Agathe Snow's *Goldfinch* (2008).

THE BASICS

www.guggenheim.org

➕ E5

✉ 1071 5th Avenue/89th Street

☎ 212/423-3500

🕐 Sun–Wed, Fri 10–5.45, Sat 10–7.45; closed Dec 25

🍴 Café

🚇 4, 5, 6 86th Street

🚌 M1, M2, M3, M4

♿ Good

💲 Expensive

❓ Lecture program; audio tours

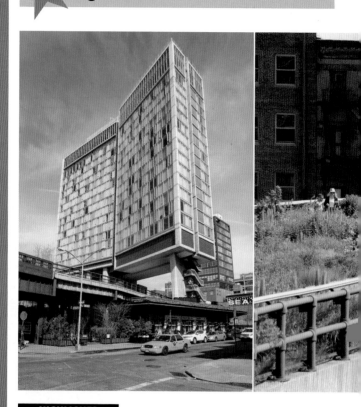

HIGHLIGHTS

- The Whitney Museum
- Site-specific art installations
- Northern spur preserve
- 10th Avenue Square

TIP

- Because the park keeps entirely to the original rail line, narrow sections can be crowded. Come early before the day heats up or enjoy a leisurely stroll just before sunset.

Just a decade ago, the High Line was a weed-choked, abandoned rail line snaking through the industrial waterfront. Today, it's a beautiful park that attracts more annual visitors than the Statue of Liberty.

Train tracks Manhattan in the 19th-century was the largest port in America, with many commercial piers lining the Hudson River. To move the huge amount of goods, Tenth Avenue was overlaid with railroad tracks so dangerous that the street was nicknamed Death Avenue. In the early 1930s, the trains were moved to a second-story elevated track running through many of the factories and warehouses, including the giant Nabisco headquarters (birthplace of the Oreo cookie) that is now Chelsea Market (▷ 121).

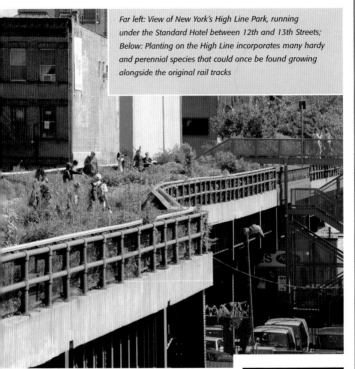

Far left: View of New York's High Line Park, running under the Standard Hotel between 12th and 13th Streets; Below: Planting on the High Line incorporates many hardy and perennial species that could once be found growing alongside the original rail tracks

Friends of the High Line After the freight line folded, the abandoned sections of track became overgrown. In 1999, Friends of the High Line formed to advocate turning this wilderness into an amenity. A park was opened and now stretches 1.45 miles (2.3km) from Gansevoort Street to West 34th Street. The park's popularity has been a boon for the surrounding neighborhood, drawing new luxury condos, hotels (like the Standard, which straddles the park) and restaurants to the area. Where the tracks cross 10th Avenue at 17th Street, seating allows visitors to gaze uptown; a few steps south, an overgrown spur track recalls what the High Line looked like before renovation work. In summer, the park hosts temporary exhibitions, and the park's southern end joins the new home of the Whitney Museum of American Art (▷ 60–61).

THE BASICS

www.thehighline.org

✠ A13, B13–16

✉ Gansevoort Street to W 34th Street between 10th and 12th avenues (staircases up to the park located every 2–3 blocks)

☎ 212/206-9922

🕐 Daily 7–11 Jun–Sep; 7–10 Apr–May, Oct–Nov; 7–7 Dec–Mar

🍴 Numerous

🚇 A, C, E 14th Street; L 8th Avenue

🚌 M11, M12, M14, M23, M34

🎫 Free

HIGHLIGHTS

● Chandeliers in the Met foyer and auditorium
● Reflecting Pool with Henry Moore's *Reclining Figure* (1965)
● Lincoln Center Out-of-Doors Festival in summer
● NY City Ballet's *Nutcracker* in December
● Chagall murals in the foyer of the Met
● Free concerts at the David Rubenstein Atrium
● New York Film Festival
● The Revson Fountain in the Central Plaza
● Jazz at Lincoln Center
● Annual *Messiah* singalong

TIP

● Dance under the stars at the Midsummer Night's Swing in Josie Robertson Plaza, a summertime series of live band sessions.

Strolling across the Central Plaza to the fantastically lit 10-story colonnade of the Metropolitan Opera House on a deep winter's night is one of the most glamorous things you can do in this city, and you don't need tickets to come and look.

West Side Story The Rockefeller-funded arts center was envisaged in the late 1950s and finished in 1969, after 7,000 families and 800 businesses had been pushed aside by city planner Robert Moses. The opening scene of *West Side Story* was filmed here after the demolition began.

All the arts The 16-acre (6ha) site includes several of New York's top arts venues, all designed by different architects in the same

Clockwise from left: The Revson Fountain, between the David H. Koch Theater (left) and the Metropolitan Opera House (right); the David Rubenstein Atrium is a great place to meet up with friends; Alice Tully Hall, one of several classical music venues; visitors to the Lincoln Center

white travertine. The Metropolitan Opera House is the glamor queen, with her vast Marc Chagall murals, red carpet, fabulous sweeping staircase and sparkling chandeliers that thrillingly rise to the gold-leaf ceiling before performances. You can take a fascinating backstage tour. David Geffen Hall is home to America's oldest orchestra, the NY Philharmonic, while the Juilliard School of Music supplies the ensemble with fresh talent. The David H. Koch Theater, housing the New York City Ballet, faces David Geffen Hall across the Plaza. The Franklin P. Rose Hall is the centerpiece of Jazz at Lincoln Center in the Time Warner Center down the street. A Broadway house, two smaller theaters, and a more intimate concert hall, Alice Tully, plus the Walter Reade movie theater and many smaller venues complete the pack.

THE BASICS

www.lincolncenter.org

⊞ B8

✉ 64th Street at Columbus Avenue

☎ Met 212/362-6000, Avery Fisher Hall 212/875-5030, Jazz 212/721-6500

🕐 Inquire for performance times

🍴 Restaurants, cafés, bars

Ⓢ 1 66th Street–Lincoln Center

🚌 M5, M7, M10, M11, M104, crosstown M66

♿ Good

💲 Center admission free

❓ Tours daily from David Rubenstein Atrium, 10.30–4.30, tel 212/875-5350

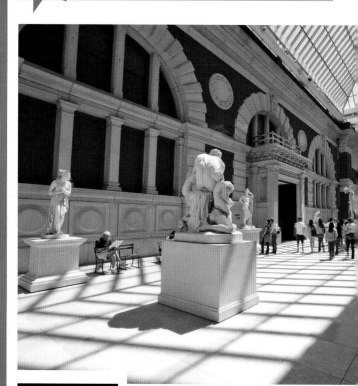

The third largest art museum in the world (after the Louvre and the Hermitage) has something for everyone, from ancient artifacts to cutting-edge fashion, arms and armor, and some of the most famous paintings in the world. It's so big that it doesn't just contain Egyptian artifacts but an entire Egyptian building.

Art city The Met's limestone Beaux Arts facade with its tremendous steps was a 1902 addition to the Calvert Vaux (of Central Park fame) red-brick Gothic building buried inside. There are several more buildings-within-buildings, interior gardens and courtyards, such is the scale of the Met. The 15BC Temple of Dendur, in its glass-walled moated chamber east of the main entrance, is the best known, but there's much

Clockwise from left: The Met's European Sculpture Court; Wheat Field with Cypresses, Vincent van Gogh (1889), the European Paintings and Sculpture Room; the Beaux Arts facade of the museum

more besides: The Astor Court above it—a replica Ming dynasty scholar's courtyard—plus, in the American Wing, a score of period-style rooms, and the vast and sunlit garden court with its hodgepodge of Tiffany glass and topiary, a Frank Lloyd Wright window and the entire Federal-style facade of the United States Bank transplanted here from Wall Street.

Where to start? How to stop? A quarter of the three million-plus objects are on display at any one time, so pace yourself. There are about 23 distinct collections. Some visitors decide to focus on one or two collections per visit, others structure a route around their favorite works. Free guided tours of the museum highlights take place daily; ask at the information desk for details.

THE BASICS

www.metmuseum.org

⊞ D5–6

✉ 1000 5th Avenue/82nd Street

☎ 212/535-7710

🕐 Sun–Thu 10–5.30, Fri–Sat 10–9

🍴 Cafeteria, restaurant, bar

🚇 4, 5, 6 86th Street

🚌 M1, M2, M3, M4

♿ Good

💲 Expensive

❓ The Cloisters (▷ 74) houses more of the Met's medieval collections; same-week admission on Met ticket

HIGHLIGHTS

- *Hope*, Klimt (1907–08)
- *Dance*, Matisse (1909)
- *Les Demoiselles d'Avignon*, Picasso (1907)
- *Starry Night*, Van Gogh (1889)
- *Gas*, Hopper (1940)
- *One: Number 31*, Pollock (1950)
- *Flag*, Jasper Johns (1954–55)
- Sculpture Garden

Yoshio Taniguchi's MoMA expansion in 2004 doubled the museum's gallery space; now, the museum is poised to grow again, providing more room to showcase its unmatched collection of everything from Postimpressionist paintings to film.

Postimpressionists to graffiti artists Founded on the 1931 bequest of Lillie P. Bliss, which comprised 235 works of art, MoMA's collections now amount to about 150,000 pieces. These include household objects, photography, graphic design, conceptual art, industrial design and media. The collection starts in the late 19th century, with the Postimpressionists and later Fauvists. Among the 20th-century movements represented in the museum are Cubism, Futurism, Expressionism, Surrealism, Abstract

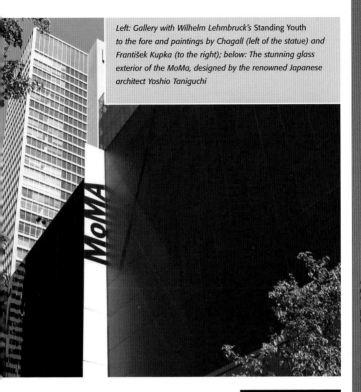

Left: Gallery with Wilhelm Lehmbruck's Standing Youth to the fore and paintings by Chagall (left of the statue) and František Kupka (to the right); below: The stunning glass exterior of the MoMa, designed by the renowned Japanese architect Yoshio Taniguchi

Expressionism, Pop (Oldenburg, Dine, Rauschenberg and Warhol) and the "Graffiti" work of Keith Haring and Jean-Michel Basquiat.

Even more modern A sunlit, 110ft (33m) high atrium affords a view of the Abby Aldrich Rockefeller Sculpture Garden, a museum favorite containing such works as Picasso's *She-Goat* (1950) and Barnett Newman's *Broken Obelisk* (1963–69). Taniguchi's building features much use of glass, granite, aluminum and light, and individual galleries have been designed specifically for the media they house. Changing exhibitions are staged on the top floor. There's a WiFi network throughout the museum, allowing visitors to download audio tours in several languages onto smart phones and other devices with HTML browsers.

THE BASICS

www.moma.org
➕ D10
✉ 11 W 53rd Street/ 5th–6th avenues
☎ 212/708-9400
🕐 Sat–Thu 10.30–5.30, Fri 10.30–8
🍴 Restaurant
Ⓔ E, M 5th Avenue–53rd Street; B, D, F 47th–50th streets–Rockefeller Center
🚌 M1, 2, 3, 4, 5, 7
♿ Good
💲 Expensive; free Fri 4–8

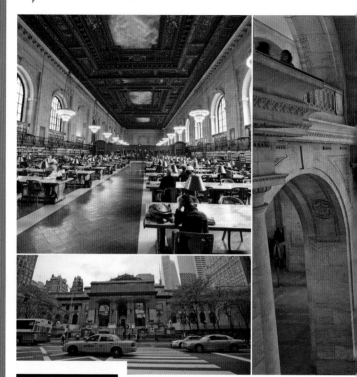

HIGHLIGHTS

● Patience and Fortitude
● Main Reading Room
● Thomas Jefferson's handwritten Declaration of Independence
● Astor Hall
● American Jewish Oral History Collection
● Gottesman Hall ceiling

TIP

● It's worth taking one of the free one-hour tours (Mon–Sat 11, 2, Sun 2). Meet at the reception desk in Astor Hall.

The New York Public Library's Central Research Building is a great white, hushed palace, beautiful to behold even if you have no time to open any of its books. It is a US National Historic Landmark.

The building Carrère and Hastings (who also designed the Frick, ▷ 32–33) were the architects of what is generally thought to be the city's best representative of the Beaux Arts style, the sumptuous yet classical French school that flourished from 1880 to 1920 in New York. In 2011 the library was discreetly rechristened the Stephen A. Schwarzman Building, after the Wall Street financier who donated $100 million towards its renovation. A pair of lions, which Mayor LaGuardia named Patience and Fortitude during the Depression, flank the stair that leads

Clockwise from far left: The Main Reading Room of the New York Public Library; Astor Hall, the starting point of guided tours; the exterior of the library, one of the finest Beaux Arts buildings in New York

into the white marble temple of Astor Hall. Inside, see temporary exhibitions in the Gottesman Hall, and look skywards: The carved oak ceiling is sublime. Priceless items from the library's collection, such as the first Gutenberg Bible brought to the New World, line the balcony corridor or are displayed in upstairs rooms. Don't miss the stunning two-block-long reading rooms, or the Richard Haas murals of NYC publishing houses in the De Witt Wallace Periodical Room.

The books The library owns more than 18 million books, most kept in the 82 branches. This building is dedicated to research. The CATNYP computer can disgorge any of the 16 million manuscripts or three million books from the 92 miles (148km) of stacks.

THE BASICS

www.nypl.org

✚ D11–12

✉ 476 5th Avenue/42nd Street

☎ 917/275-6975

🕐 Mon, Thu–Sat 10–6, Tue–Wed 10–8, Sun 1–5; closed public holidays

🍴 Kiosks outside (summer)

🚇 4, 5, 6, S Grand Central–42nd Street, 7 5th Avenue

🚌 M1, M2, M3, M4, M5, M7, M42

🚆 Metro North, Grand Central

♿ Good

🆓 Free

TIP

● There's a vast array of
shops, casual restaurants,
and more in a basement
arcade below the center.
There's a great vantage for
watching winter skaters
down there, too.

This complex of art deco buildings provides
many of those "Gee, this is New York"
moments, especially at Christmas when you
can watch ice-skaters ringed by the flags of
the UN and gaze up at the massive tree.

Prometheus **is here** The 19-building
Rockefeller Center has been called the
greatest urban complex of the 20th century.
John D. Rockefeller Jr.'s grand real estate
scheme provided work for 40,000 people
during the Depression. Its centerpiece
is the elongated ziggurat GE Building (formerly
the RCA building) at 30 Rockefeller Plaza,
adorned with Lee Lawrie's glass-and-limestone
frieze, lobby murals by José Maria Sert and
various other artworks. Rest for a while on a
Channel Gardens bench and gaze on the Lower

Clockwise from far left: Radio City Music Hall forms part of Rockefeller Center; Paul Manship's bronze Prometheus (1934) on the Lower Plaza; Friendship Between America and France (1934), a gilded bronze by Alfred Janniot above the Fifth Avenue entrance

Plaza, the ice rink and Paul Manship's gilded bronze *Prometheus* (1934).

Top of the Rock The three-tiered observation deck at the top of the GE building affords stunning panoramic views over Manhattan and the only public overview of Central Park. The mezzanine museum tells the history of the complex before high-speed elevators whisk you to the 67th–70th floor viewing platforms.

NBC and Rockettes The GE Building also houses NBC Studios. Take a studio tour or join the line for standby tickets for *Saturday Night Live*. Over on Avenue of the Americas is Radio City Music Hall, home to the Rockettes, who star in the annual Christmas Spectacular, one of the top shows in town.

THE BASICS

www.rockefellercenter.com
🚹 D10–11, E10–11
✉ 5th–6th avenues/ 48th–51st streets
☎ 212/632-3975
🕐 Various
🍴 Many restaurants, cafés
Ⓑ B, D, F, M 47th–50th streets–Rockefeller Center
🚌 M1, M2, M3, M4, M5, M7, M50
♿ Moderate
💲 Free
❓ Radio City tours, tel 212/247-4777; NBC Studio tours, tel 212/664-3700; Rockefeller Center tours, tel 212/698-2000

Top of the Rock
www.topoftherocknyc.com
☎ 212/698-2000
🕐 Daily 8am–midnight (last elevator 11pm)
💲 Expensive

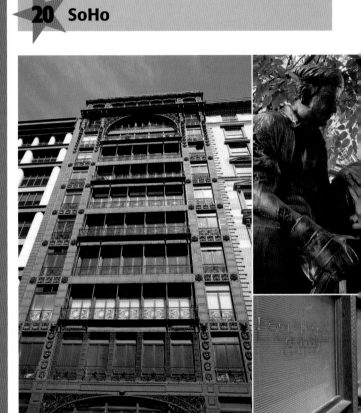

HIGHLIGHTS

- Shopping
- King and Queen of Greene Street
- Little Singer Building
- Haughwout Building

TIP

- Stop at Dean & DeLuca (Broadway and Prince) for a coffee and pastry, a hot sandwich, or to browse its delectable gourmet fare, including its cheese and dessert counters.

In the last 150 years, SoHo has come full circle. New York's toniest shopping district around the time of the Civil War, the area fell on hard times by World War II. Now, its landmark cast-iron buildings teem with trendy shops again.

Cast in iron An acronym for "South of Houston," SoHo stretches for several delightful blocks between Houston and Canal streets, bordered by Lafayette Street on the east and Sixth Avenue to the west. Around 500 of its 19th-century industrial buildings have been preserved in the SoHo Cast Iron Historic District. Cast-iron architecture was not only strong and fire-resistant, but enabled ornate buildings in Italianate and other elaborate styles to be erected quickly and cheaply. Some of the finest

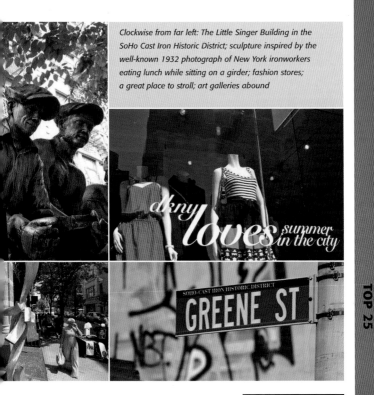

Clockwise from far left: The Little Singer Building in the SoHo Cast Iron Historic District; sculpture inspired by the well-known 1932 photograph of New York ironworkers eating lunch while sitting on a girder; fashion stores; a great place to stroll; art galleries abound

examples are the King (No. 72) and Queen (No. 28) of Greene Street, the Little Singer Building (561 Broadway) and also the Haughwout Building (488 Broadway), which had the first Otis steam elevator. Old-fashioned lampposts further enhance SoHo's charm.

Art and fashion By the 1960s and '70s, many of SoHo's commercial buildings were abandoned. Then, artists moved in, art galleries followed, and SoHo became the hippest quarter in town. Rising prices forced many artists and galleries to Chelsea and beyond, but fashionistas quickly filled the empty and spacious showrooms. Everything from Prada's flagship store to branches of Bloomingdale's and London's Topshop to designer boutiques make this a shopper's heaven.

THE BASICS

- E18–19
- Houston–Canal streets, Lafayette Street–6th Avenue
- Numerous
- N, R Prince Street; 6 Spring Street; C, E Spring Street
- M5, M21
- Good

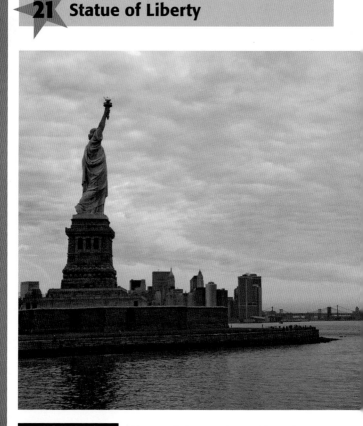

HIGHLIGHTS

● View from the crown
● Statue of Liberty Museum
● Fort Wood, the star-shaped pedestal base
● The refurbished torch

TIP

● Visits to the crown must be reserved well in advance (sometimes months) on tel 201/604-2800 or online at www.statuecruises.com. There are no same-day crown tickets.

Liberty Enlightening the World (as she's formally known), symbol of the American dream of freedom, takes your breath away, however many times you've seen her image—and despite her modest stature.

How she grew In the late 1860s, sculptor Frédéric-Auguste Bartholdi dreamed of placing a monument to freedom in a prominent location. His dream merged with the French historian Edouard-René de Laboulaye's idea of presenting the American people with a statue that celebrated freedom and the two nations' friendship. Part of the idea was to shame the repressive French government, but, apparently, New Yorkers took their freedom for granted. It was only after Joseph Pulitzer promised to print the name of every donor in his newspaper, the

Clockwise from far left: Liberty Island, a beacon of hope since 1886; Liberty's seven-pointed crown; the symbol of American liberty raises her torch to the world

New York World, that citizens coughed up the funds to build the pedestal. Liberty was unveiled by President Grover Cleveland on October 28, 1886.

Mother of exiles Beneath her 25-foot-long (7.6m) feet, she tramples the shackles of tyranny, and her seven-pointed crown beams liberty to the seven continents and the seven seas. Gustave Eiffel designed the 1,700-bar iron and steel structure that supports her. She weighs 225 tons, is 151ft (46m) tall, and is covered in 300 copper plates. The torch tip towers 305ft (93m) above sea level. Emma Lazarus's stirring poem *The New Colossus* is on a plaque in the museum in the statue's base. A tablet reads: July IV MDCCLXXVI—the date of the Declaration of Independence.

THE BASICS

www.nps.gov/stli
➕ See map ▷ 110
✉ Liberty Island
☎ 212/363-3200
🕐 Daily 9.30–5; extended hours in peak season. A limited number of daily tickets to tour the pedestal/museum may be reserved in advance from ferry office, by phone or online
🍴 Cafeteria
Ⓜ 4, 5 Bowling Green, 1 South Ferry, then take ferry
🚍 M5, M15, M20 South Ferry, then take ferry
🚢 Departs Battery Park
☎ 877/523-9849; www.statuecruises.com
♿ Poor
💲 Free; ferry expensive

TOP 25

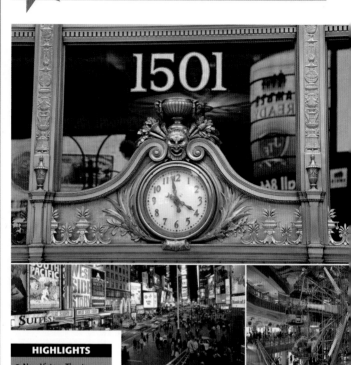

- New Victory Theater
- Shubert Alley
- Indoor Ferris wheel at Toys R Us
- ABC's *Good Morning* studio: 44th/Broadway
- New Year's Eve ball drop

TIP

- The TKTS booth, located at Duffy Square, 47th Street/Broadway, sells same-day theater tickets for 20–50 percent off. The booth is open daily 3–8 for evening shows (from 2pm Tue), Wed and Sat 10–2 for matinees, Sun 11–7 for all shows.

"The Crossroads of the World," one-time symbol of Manhattan glitz and glam, is an area New Yorkers love to hate—especially since it has been sanitized. You may disagree as you explore the big stores and are dazzled by the neon.

Longacre Square The junction of Broadway and Seventh Avenue was called Longacre Square until Times Tower, the new home of the *New York Times*, was finished in 1904. Almost immediately, the relocation of the theater district, the opening of the first subway and the decision to site the New Year celebration here conspired to make it the de facto center of Manhattan.

On Broadway The theaters moved in to the area, and Broadway, the Great White Way,

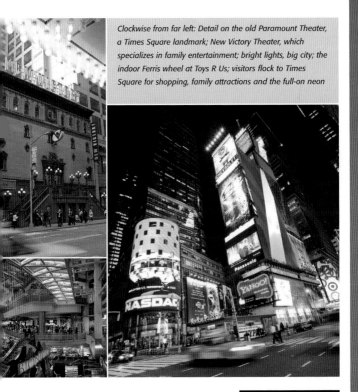

Clockwise from far left: Detail on the old Paramount Theater, a Times Square landmark; New Victory Theater, which specializes in family entertainment; bright lights, big city; the indoor Ferris wheel at Toys R Us; visitors flock to Times Square for shopping, family attractions and the full-on neon

became synonymous with bigtime showbiz with its popular theatrical—especially musical—division. By 1914 there were some 43 theaters in the immediate vicinity of the square; after multiple closures, refurbishments and reopenings, there are 40 of them today.

Best of Times, worst of Times By the 1970s Times Square was decaying, many of the legitimate theaters having fallen on hard times and become porn theaters. But a massive clean-up effort in the 1990s brought about the area's rebirth. Today it's a tourist hotspot, with a raft of family attractions, megastores and restaurants beneath the glittering state-of-the-art illuminations. A large section of Times Square is now car-free, though the human traffic jams are bigger than ever.

THE BASICS

www.timessquarenyc.org

🚇 D11

🚉 1, 2, 3, 7, N, Q, R, S Times Square–42nd Street

🚌 M5, M7, M20, M42, M104

❓ An audio-enhanced walking tour leaves several times daily from The Actors' Chapel (239 West 49th Street).
TKTS Booth: www.tdf.org/nyc/81/TKTS-Live provides real-time updates of what is on offer before you commit to standing in line

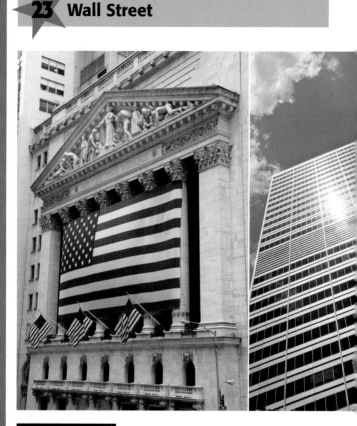

HIGHLIGHTS

● Trinity Church
● Federal Hall
● New York Stock Exchange
● "The House of Morgan"

TIP

● Stand on the top step of Federal Hall to recreate the famous photo of the New York Stock Exchange, shot over the shoulder of the statue of George Washington.

Depending on your point of view, Wall Street is the boon or bane of the world's economic fortunes. But either way, the historic buildings and urban buzz of this financial powerhouse are fascinating to see and experience.

The Buttonwood Agreement Wall Street, named for the Dutch colonial wall that once marked the city's northern boundary, is the epicenter of the financial district. It has been so since the late 18th century, when businessmen gathered here under a buttonwood tree to trade bonds, issued to finance debts incurred in the Revolutionary War. In 1792, 24 traders signed the Buttonwood Agreement, which created the New York Stock Exchange. Today the NYSE is the largest stock exchange in the

Clockwise from far left: The New York Stock Exchange; the soaring towers of Wall Street; Federal Hall, fronted by a bronze statue of George Washington and modeled on the Greek Parthenon; the beautifully decorated domed ceiling in the entrance of Federal Hall

world. The 1903 building, with its grand trading floor and facade of Corinthian columns, stands at the corner with Broad Street.

A million-dollar stroll At the west end of Wall Street stands Trinity Church (1846), the third on this site. The original, built in 1699, was the city's first church. Alexander Hamilton and other famous New Yorkers are buried in the church-yard. At the corner of Wall and Broad streets sits the "House of Morgan," once the most powerful financial institution in America (now housing apartments). George Washington was sworn in as America's first president at Federal Hall, now a national memorial and museum. Forty Wall Street is owned by Donald Trump. At No. 48, the Museum of American Finance has displays on financial history.

THE BASICS

www.downtownny.com
www.nps.gov/feha
www.moaf.org
www.trinitywallstreet.org

➕ E22

✉ NYSE, 18 Broad Street; Federal Hall, 26 Wall Street; Museum of American Finance, 48 Wall Street; Trinity Church, Broadway at Wall Street

☎ Federal Hall 212/825-6990; Museum of American Finance 212/908-4110; Trinity Church 212/602-0800

🕐 Federal Hall Mon–Fri 9–5; Museum of American Finance Tue–Sat 10–4; Trinity Church Mon–Fri 7–6, Sat 8–4, Sun 7–4

🍴 Restaurants, pubs

🚇 2, 3, 4, 5 Wall Street; J, Z Broad Street 🚌 M5

♿ Federal Hall free; Museum of American Finance moderate; Trinity Church free

❓ Tours: Download Trinity Church's guided tour app from their website.

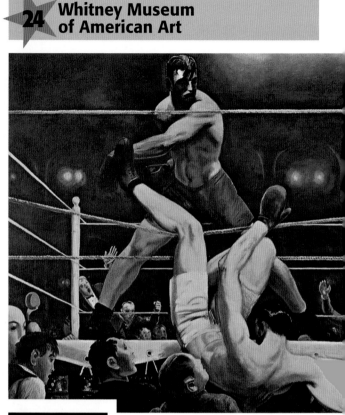

HIGHLIGHTS

● Whitney Biennial
● *Brooklyn Bridge*, Joseph Stella (1939)
● Hoppers
● O'Keeffes
● *Dempsey and Firpo*, George Bellows (1924)
● Louise Nevelsons

TIP

● Download the audio-visual smartphone app from the Whitney's website before you go and use it to enhance your visit at the museum.

Gertrude Vanderbilt Whitney's world-class collection, a showcase of her work and that of her friends, was first shown in a modest Greenwich Village studio space in 1918. Today, the collection is housed in the stunning and innovative Renzo Piano-designed head-quarters along the High Line.

No room at the Met Sculptor and patron of her contemporaries' work, Gertrude Vanderbilt Whitney offered her collection to the Met in 1929, but the great institution turned up its nose. Whitney instead formalized her own museum space, first in the Village, and then from 1966 to 2014 in Marcel Breuer's cantilevered headquarters on the Upper East Side. Having outgrown that space (now, ironically, in the process of becoming an

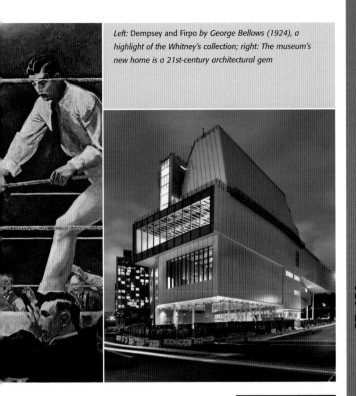

Left: Dempsey and Firpo *by George Bellows (1924), a highlight of the Whitney's collection; right: The museum's new home is a 21st-century architectural gem*

offshoot of the Met), the museum moved in 2015 to Renzo Piano's dramatic new building in the Meatpacking District. The Whitney's collection reads like a roll call of American 20th-century greats: Edward Hopper, Thomas Hart Benton, Willem de Kooning, Georgia O'Keeffe, Claes Oldenburg, Jasper Johns, George Bellows and Jackson Pollock are a few.

Take your pick Exhibitions, drawn from the museum's permanent collection, often emphasize a single artist's work. At other times they prove more eclectic. The Whitney Biennial (in the spring of even-numbered years) presents the curator's vision—sometimes controversial—of the leading trends in American art during the past two years and often features the work of young or lesser-known artists.

THE BASICS

www.whitney.org

🚹 B16

✉ 99 Gansevoort Street/ Washington Street

☎ 212/570-3600

🕐 Sun, Mon, Wed 10.30–6, Thu–Sat 10.30–10

🍴 Restaurant, café

🚇 A, C, E 14th Street; L 8th Avenue

🚌 M14

♿ Excellent

💲 Expensive (under 18s free); donation Fri 7–10pm

❓ Free daily tours

25 World Trade Center

HIGHLIGHTS

● Memorial waterfalls
● One World Observatory
● 9/11 Museum
● One World Trade Center
● Transportation hub

TIP

● Admission to the above-ground memorial is free at all times, but a ticket is required to visit the museum below.

The twin towers of the World Trade Center, once the tallest buildings in the world, were a New York icon until they were destroyed by terrorists who crashed two hijacked planes into them on September 11, 2001. From the ashes, a moving memorial has risen that pays tribute to those who lost their lives in the tragedy.

The National September 11 Memorial and Museum An international contest was held to select a fitting memorial for the site. Architects Michael Arad and Peter Walker's design, entitled "Reflecting Absence," was chosen. It comprises two square waterfalls, situated over the foot-print of the towers. The waterfalls cascade 30ft (9m) into pools that disappear into a center void. The pools are surrounded by bronze

Clockwise from far left: Waterfalls at the National September 11 Memorial; One World Observatory; red and white roses on one of the inscribed bronze panels around the reflecting pools; the National September 11 Memorial from above

panels inscribed with the names of almost 3,000 known victims of both this and a bomb attack on the towers in 1993. A memorial park with more than 300 oak trees provides a peaceful space for contemplation. The museum features a history of the site and relics from the original World Trade Center, including the last column of steel to be removed from the rubble.

One World Observatory Atop One World Trade Center (presently America's tallest building) is One World Observatory, with 360-degree views of Manhattan, Brooklyn, New York Harbor, and beyond. "Sky Pods" (elevators) whisk visitors up to the 100th-story view in 60 seconds. Staff are available to answer questions about the landmarks that can be seen, such as Santiago Calatrava's winged transportation hub.

THE BASICS

➕ D21

✉ Church–West streets, Vesey–Liberty streets

☎ Memorial and Museum: 212/266-5211

🕐 Memorial: daily 7.30am–9pm; Museum: Sun–Thu 9–8 (last entry at 6), Fri–Sat 9–9 (last entry at 7); Observatory: daily 9–8; longer in summer

🚇 E World Trade Center, A, C, J, Z, 2, 3, 4, 5 Fulton Street

🚌 M5, M20, M22

♿ Good

🎟 Memorial free; Museum expensive; Observatory expensive

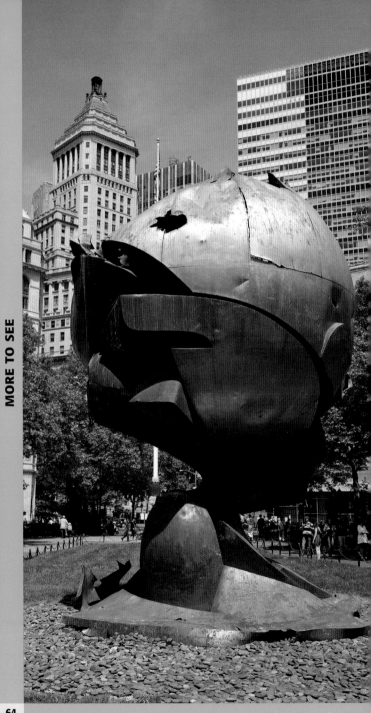

More to See

This section contains other great places to visit if you have more time. Some are in the heart of the city while others are a short journey away, found under Farther Afield. This chapter also has fantastic excursions that you should set aside a whole day to visit.

MORE TO SEE

In the Heart of the City

AMERICAN FOLK ART MUSEUM

www.folkartmuseum.org

The outstanding collection of quilts is a highlight in this museum spanning the rich variety of folk art, from paintings and pottery to textiles and woodcarving, and dating from the 18th century to the present day. The museum's shop stocks a superb range of handcrafted items.

🔁 C8 ✉ 2 Lincoln Square (Columbus Avenue between 65th and 66th Streets) ☎ 212/595-9533 🕐 Tue–Sat 11.30–7, Sun 12–6 🚇 1 66th Street–Lincoln Center 🎟 Free

BATTERY PARK

www.thebattery.org

At the southernmost tip of Manhattan, with splendid views of New York Harbor, Battery Park was named for the cannon sited here to defend the fledgling city against British attack. Ferries to the Statue of Liberty and Ellis Island leave from Castle Clinton National Monument, a former fort. Among the monuments in the park, look for *The Sphere*, which once stood at the World Trade Center plaza and serves as a memorial to 9/11.

🔁 E23 ✉ Tip of Manhattan 🚇 1 South Ferry; 4, 5 Bowling Green

BROOKLYN BRIDGE

Completed in 1883, the Brooklyn Bridge was the first to link Manhattan and Brooklyn. With its twin Gothic towers and graceful ballet of cables, it is one of New York's finest landmarks. Stroll across the pedestrian walkway for views of the Manhattan skyline.

🔁 G21 🚇 4, 5, 6 Brooklyn Bridge–City Hall; A, C High Street/Brooklyn Bridge

CHELSEA

North of Greenwich Village is the neighborhood of Chelsea. Its landmark Chelsea Hotel (222 W 23rd Street), made famous in Andy Warhol's film *Chelsea Girls*, was home to a roll-call of artists, musicians and writers including Thomas Wolfe, Dylan Thomas, Arthur Miller and Arthur C. Clarke, who wrote *2001: A Space Odyssey* here. The Chelsea Art District, from 19th to

The American Folk Art Museum

Chelsea Hotel, a favorite haunt of artists, writers and musicians

29th streets west of 10th avenue, has eclipsed SoHo with its numerous galleries. Also worth seeing: Chelsea Market (▷ 121), the Chelsea Piers sports complex on the Hudson River (enter on 23rd Street), the High Line (▷ 40) and the Rubin Museum of Art (▷ 71). 🚇 A–D13–15 ✉ From 30th Street south to 14th Street, and 6th Avenue west to the Hudson River 🚇 1, 14th, 18th, 23rd, 28th streets–7th Avenue; C, E 14th, 23rd streets–8th Avenue

CHRYSLER BUILDING

The gleaming art deco spire of the Chrysler Building is an iconic symbol of New York. When completed in 1931, it held the title of "world's tallest building" until it was surpassed by the Empire State Building the same year. Every detail of the 77-story building evokes a 1929 Chrysler Plymouth. The winged steel gargoyles are modeled on its radiator caps; the building's stepped setbacks carry stylized hubcaps and the spire resembles a radiator grille. You can visit the lobby to see the art deco

The Chrysler Building

detailing in the red marble, granite and chrome interior, surmounted by the 97ft by 100ft (30m by 31m) mural depicting industrial scenes and celebrating "transportation." Don't miss the art deco marquetry on the elevator doors. 🚇 F11 ✉ 405 Lexington Avenue/42nd Street 🕐 Mon–Fri office hours; closed public holidays 🚇 4, 5, 6, 7, S Grand Central–42nd Street 🚌 M101, M102, M103, M42 🚃 Metro North, Grand Central ♿ Good 🎫 Free

CITY HALL

http://www.nyc.gov/html/artcom
Built between 1803 and 1812 in Federal and French Renaissance styles, this is one of the nation's oldest city halls. The building and the rotunda, with its Corinthian columns and coffered dome, are designated landmarks. See the Governor's Room furniture and portrait collection on a guided tour. 🚇 E21 ✉ Broadway/Murray Street ☎ 311 or 212/639-9675 🕐 Wed (admission on a first come, first served basis) and Thu (advance reservations required) 🚇 2, 3 Park Place; 4, 5, 6 Brooklyn Bridge–City Hall; R City Hall 🎫 Free

ELDRIDGE STREET SYNAGOGUE

www.eldridgestreet.org
Built in 1887, this synagogue is a symbol of the aspirations of Eastern European immigrants on the Lower East Side. Its 50ft (15m) vaulted ceiling, Moorish and Romanesque details, and stained-glass windows make it one of the city's architectural gems. Exhibits and guided tours point out design features and tell the story of this diverse neighborhood.

⊞ G19 ✉ 12 Eldridge Street
☎ 212/219-0302 ⏰ Sun–Thu 10–5, Fri
10–3 🚇 F East Broadway; B, D Grand
Street 🎟 Moderate

FLATIRON BUILDING

This 1902 skyscraper designed by
Daniel Burnham was named for its
amazing and memorable shape. It
is an isosceles triangle with a sharp
angle pointing uptown.
⊞ E14 ✉ 175 5th Avenue/E 22nd–23rd
streets 🚇 N, R 23rd Street

GRACE CHURCH

www.gracechurchnyc.org
This James Renwick-designed
Gothic Revival church dating from
the mid-19th century has superb
stained glass and a mosaic floor.
⊞ E–F16 ✉ 802 Broadway ☎ 212/254-
2000 ⏰ Mon–Sat 12–5, Sun services
🚇 N, R 8th Street–NYU; 6 Astor Place
🎟 Free guided tours Sun 1pm

ITALIAN AMERICAN MUSEUM

www.italianamericanmuseum.org
In the heart of Little Italy, this small
museum explores the history of
the quarter and the rich heritage
of its Italian immigrants. Exhibits
range from New York policeman
Frank Serpico's guns to a collection
of marionettes from the 1920s
and 1930s.
⊞ F19 ✉ 155 Mulberry Street/Grand
Street ☎ 212/965-9000 ⏰ Mon–Fri by
appointment, Sat 11–6, Sun 12–6
🚇 N, R Prince Street; F, V Broadway–
Lafayette 🎟 Donation

JEWISH MUSEUM

www.thejewishmuseum.org
The largest Jewish museum in the
Western hemisphere chronicles
Jewish experience worldwide.
Artifacts in the permanent collec-
tion cover 4,000 years of Jewish
history, while special exhibitions
focus on Jewish culture and more.
⊞ E4 ✉ 1109 5th Avenue/92nd Street
☎ 212/423-3200 ⏰ Sat–Tue 11–5.45,
Thu 11–8, Fri (Mar–Oct) 11–5.45 🍴 Café
🚇 4, 5, 6 86th Street 🎟 Moderate; free Sat

LOWER EAST SIDE
TENEMENT MUSEUM

www.tenement.org
This reconstruction of life in an
1863 tenement block is a must for

The Italian American Museum documents the rich history of Little Italy

history buffs. A choice of tours focus on the homes and workshops of Jewish, Italian and Irish immigrants, and there are also walking tours of the neighborhood. All the tours leave from the museum shop.

🔢 G18 ✉ 103 Orchard Street
☎ 212/982-8420 ⏰ Tours daily 10–5, visitor center Fri–Wed 10–6.30, Thu 10–8.30
🚇 F, J, M, Z Delancey Street–Essex Street; B, D Grand Street 💲 Expensive

MEATPACKING DISTRICT

www.meatpacking-district.com
Bordered roughly by Jane and W 14th streets west of Greenwich Street/Ninth Avenue, this interesting district of cobbled streets was named for its wholesale meat warehouses. It is now filled with hot nightclubs and trendy, late-night restaurants. Come after dark to see what all the fuss is about, unless you want to shop in its designer boutiques, from Christian Louboutin to Scoop—or to visit the Whitney Museum of American Art (▷ 60).

🔢 C15 🚇 A, C, E 14th Street

MORGAN LIBRARY & MUSEUM

www.themorgan.org
This collection of literary works, rare musical manuscripts and artworks is one of the finest in the world. Highlights here include the ninth-century Lindau Gospels, a vellum copy of the Gutenberg Bible, music scores by Beethoven, Mozart and Puccini, etchings by Raphael and Michelangelo and manuscripts by Charles Dickens and Mark Twain.

🔢 E12 ✉ 225 Madison Avenue/E 36th Street ☎ 212/685-0008 ⏰ Tue–Thu 10.30–5, Fri 10.30–9, Sat 10–6, Sun 11–6
🚇 6 33rd Street; 4, 5, 6 7 Grand Central
💲 Expensive

EL MUSEO DEL BARRIO

www.elmuseo.org
This museum dedicated to Latin American and Caribbean art contains over 8,000 items from pre-Columbian artifacts to modern paintings and photographs. There is also a program of events.

🔢 E2 ✉ 1230 5th Avenue/104th Street
☎ 212/831-7272 ⏰ Tue–Sat 11–6
🚇 6 103rd Street 💲 Moderate

New York's Jewish Museum chronicles the history of Jews worldwide

MORE TO SEE

MUSEUM OF ARTS AND DESIGN

www.madmuseum.org

Affectionaly known as "MAD," the museum showcases crafts, art, and design through an impressive permanent collection and special exhibitions. A biennial showcases "NYC Makers," highlighting the work of artists and artisans across all five boroughs.

➕ C9 ✉ 2 Columbus Circle ☎ 212/299-2777 🕐 Sat–Sun, Tue–Wed 10–6, Thu–Fri 10–9 🍴 Restaurant 🚇 1, A, C, B, D 59th Street–Columbus Circle 💰 Expensive (by donation Thu 6–9pm)

MUSEUM OF THE CITY OF NEW YORK

www.mcny.org

Rotating exhibitions here illustrate the ever-changing life of the city since 1624. It has an outstanding collection of photographs, as well as toys, furniture and decorative arts. Special walking tours are available also.

➕ E2 ✉ 1220 5th Avenue/103rd Street ☎ 212/534-1672 🕐 Daily 10–6 🚇 6 103rd Street 💰 Expensive

NEUE GALERIE

www.neuegalerie.org

Dedicated to early 20th-century German and Austrian art and design, this marvelous gallery includes Gustav Klimt's portrait known as *Golden Adele*. Many other artists are represented including Max Beckmann and Ernst Ludwig Kirchener.

➕ E5 ✉ 1048 5th Avenue/86th Street ☎ 212/628-6200 🕐 Thu–Mon 11–6 🍴 Café 🚇 4, 5, 6 86th Street 💰 Expensive

NEW MUSEUM OF CONTEMPORARY ART

www.newmuseum.org

The dynamic building resembling giant white boxes stacked askew is a fitting home for this cutting-edge museum of contemporary art. When you are done looking at the art, the seventh-floor balcony affords panoramic views of Lower Manhattan.

➕ F18 ✉ 235 Bowery/Prince Street ☎ 212/219-1222 🕐 Wed–Sun 11–6, Thu 11–9 🍴 Café 🚇 N, R Prince Street 💰 Expensive

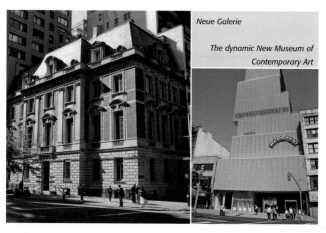

Neue Galerie

The dynamic New Museum of Contemporary Art

NEW-YORK HISTORICAL SOCIETY

www.nyhistory.org

With 1.6 million objects dating from the Dutch Colonial era to the tragic events of 9/11, the society's permanent collection and temporary exhibitions reveal key chapters in New York's past. Admission includes the film New York Story, an immersive, 18-minute narrative of the city's growth from Dutch trading port to world economic powerhouse. Many key objects are on view just inside the main entrance, including fragments from America's first capitol building and the shackles from a child who was held in slavery.

🚹 C6 ✉ Central Park West/77th Street ☎ 212/873-3400 🕐 Tue–Thu and Sat 10–6, Fri 10–8, Sun 10–5; closed public holidays 🚇 B/C 81st Street 💲 Expensive

PALEY CENTER FOR MEDIA

www.paleycenter.org

The museum's archive of 160,000 TV shows, radio programs, and commercials spans nearly 100 years. The center hosts discussions of television (past and present) as well as screenings. You can track down your favorite long-lost TV show in the catalogue and watch it on an individual monitor.

🚹 D10 ✉ 25 West 52nd Street between 5th and 6th ☎ 212/621-6800 🕐 Wed and Fri–Sun 12–6, Thu 12–8; check schedule for theater programs 🚇 E, M 5th Avenue–53rd Street 💲 Moderate

RUBIN MUSEUM OF ART

www.rubinmuseum.org

The superb collection of art from Tibet and the Himalayan region is the largest in the West. Religious art and cultural artifacts include scroll paintings, sculptures, ritual objects, textiles, masks and prints.

🚹 D15 ✉ 150 W 17th Street/Seventh Avenue ☎ 212/620-5000 🕐 Mon, Thu 11–5, Wed 11–9, Fri 11–10, Sat–Sun 11–6 🍽 Café 🚇 1 18th Street–7th Avenue 💲 Expensive, free Fri 6–10

ST. PATRICK'S CATHEDRAL

www.saintpatrickscathedral.org

With its ornate spires soaring 330ft (100m) above Fifth Avenue, James Renwick's Gothic Revival cathedral, built in 1858–79, seats

MORE TO SEE

The New York Historical Society

Revisit old commercials and TV and radio programs at the Paley Center for Media

2,200 people. The St. Michael and St. Louis altar was designed by Tiffany & Co., while the rose window is one of stained-glass artist Charles Connick's finest creations.

➕ E10 ✉ 5th Avenue between E 50th and E 51st streets ☎ 212/753-2261 🕐 Daily 6.30am–8.45pm; services at various times 🚇 6 51st Street; E, M 5th Avenue–53rd Street 🎟 Free

ST. PATRICK'S OLD CATHEDRAL

www.oldcathedral.org

New York's first Roman Catholic cathedral opened in 1815, when the area was settled by Irish immigrants. The building, restored in 1868, has a stunning hand-carved altarpiece filled with statuary.

➕ F18 ✉ Mott Street between Prince and Houston streets ☎ 212/226-8075 (call for times) 🕐 Daily 8–5 but hours may vary 🚇 N, R, Prince Street 🎟 Free

ST. PAUL'S CHAPEL

www.trinitywallstreet.org

Opened in 1766, this is the only remaining Colonial-era church to be found in Manhattan. George Washington worshiped here after his inauguration. St. Paul's escaped destruction on 9/11 and became a round-the-clock refuge for rescue workers. In the churchyard is the Bell of Hope, a gift from the City of London on the first anniversary of the tragedy.

➕ E21 ✉ 209 Broadway at Fulton Street ☎ 212/602-0800 🕐 Mon–Sat 10–6, churchyard 10–4, Sun 7–6 🚇 2, 3, 4, 5, A, C, J, Z Fulton Street 🎟 Free

SOUTH STREET SEAPORT

www.southstreetseaport.com

In the midst of a post-Hurricane Sandy transformation, South Street Seaport is smaller than it once was, but still worth exploring. The collection of the South Street Seaport Museum includes a number of historic ships. There are numerous dining and shopping options here and an outpost of the Times Square TKTS ticket booth (▷ 56) with a much smaller line than its uptown sibling.

➕ G21 ✉ Fulton Street at Water Street ☎ Museum 212/748-8600 🚇 2, 3 ,4 ,5 , A, C, J , Z to Fulton Street

The flags of member nations flying high at the United Nations Headquarters

TRUMP TOWER

Ride the escalators to admire the 1980s glitz and glamor in all its glory. The six-story atrium is filled with shops, greenery and waterfalls, while the top floors include "The Donald's" penthouse and the boardroom used in the US version of *The Apprentice* television show.

➕ E9 ✉ 725 Fifth Avenue/56th Street ☎ 212/832-2000 🕐 Daily 8am–10pm 🍴 Several 🚇 N, Q, R 5th Avenue–59th Street; E, M, 5th Avenue–53rd Street

UNION SQUARE

Named for the union of Broadway and Fourth Avenue, this is where downtown and uptown meet. It is ringed with shops and restaurants and four days a week has the city's best greenmarket, selling home-grown produce (▷ 125).

➕ E15 ✉ E 14th–17th streets, Park Avenue South, Broadway 🕐 Greenmarket Mon, Wed, Fri, Sat 8–6 🍴 Numerous 🚇 4, 5, 6, L, N, Q, R 14th Street–Union Square 🚌 M3 ♿ Good

UNITED NATIONS HEADQUARTERS

www.visit.un.org

Take a guided tour to see the General Assembly Hall and collection of art and artifacts donated from around the world. A limited number of same-day tickets are available on site, but it's much better to buy them online in advance. Arrive at least 30 minutes early for security screening.

➕ G11 ✉ 1st Avenue/45th–46th streets ☎ 212/963-8687 🕐 Mon–Fri 9.15–4.15 (A guided tour ticket is required) 🍴 Café, restaurant 🚇 4, 5, 6, 7 to Grand Central 💲 Expensive

U.S. CUSTOM HOUSE

http://www.nmai.si.edu/visit/newyork/

Also known as the Alexander Hamilton U.S. Custom House, this 1907 Beaux Arts beauty, designed by Cass Gilbert, now houses the Smithsonian's National Museum of the American Indian, highlighting native cultures of North, Central and South America.

➕ E23 ✉ 1 Bowling Green ☎ 212/514-3700 🕐 Museum daily 10–5 🚇 4, 5 Bowling Green; 1 South Ferry 💲 Free

WASHINGTON SQUARE

www.nycgovparks.org/parks/washington-square-park

The square is a prime people-watching spot in Greenwich Village. At the north end, Washington Memorial Arch, designed by Stanford White, marks the start of Fifth Avenue. Notice "The Row" of Greek Revival homes (Nos. 1–13) where the elite of 19th-century New York lived. If you want to get a real feel, read Henry James's *Washington Square*.

➕ E17 🚇 N, R 8th Street–NYU; A, B, C, D, E, F, M 4th Street–Washington Square

The U.S. Custom House

Farther Afield

BRONX ZOO

www.bronxzoo.com

The biggest city zoo in the US has over 4,000 animals and is a leader in wildlife conservation. Don't miss the Congo Gorilla Forest, or the Wild Asia Complex with its monorail riding high above tigers, rhinos and elephants.

🚇 See map ▷ 111 ⊠ Fordham Road (Bronx River Parkway Northeast) ☎ 718/367-1010 🕐 Apr–Oct daily 10–5; Nov–Mar 10–4.30 🍴 Restaurant 🚇 2 Pelham Parkway 💷 Expensive (Wed discounts)

THE CLOISTERS

www.metmuseum.org/visit/visit-the-cloisters/

A 12th-century Spanish apse attached to a Romanesque cloister and a Gothic chapel—what's all this doing in Upper Manhattan? This is the Met's medieval branch. The bulk of the art and architecture, which is arranged chronologically, was amassed by sculptor George Gray Barnard in the early 20th century. Much was rescued from ruin. The effigy of the Crusader Jean d'Alluye, for instance, was doing duty as a bridge, while the priceless Unicorn Tapestries were acting as frost blankets.

🚇 See map ▷ 111 ⊠ Fort Tryon Park, North Manhattan ☎ 212/923-3700 🕐 Mar–Oct daily 10–5.15; Nov–Feb 10–4.45; closed public holidays 🚇 A 190th Street 💷 Expensive (Met Museum admission includes entry to the Cloisters)

CONEY ISLAND

www.coneyisland.com

At the end of the 19th century, Coney Island on a peak day played host to a million people. Since then, attractions have come and gone, but the big-dipper ride, the Cyclone, is still here and Nathan's Famous hot dogs are still sold from the original site. A newer attraction is MCU Park, home of the Brooklyn Cyclones baseball team, which also hosts concerts. Also on Coney Island is the New York Aquarium. A slew of new amusement parks are revitalizing the area and restoring its charm.

🚇 See map ▷ 110 ⊠ Surf Avenue, Boardwalk; Aquarium: W 8th Street, Surf

Bronx Zoo, the largest city zoo in the US

One of the Unicorn Tapestries, a highlight of The Cloisters, the medieval branch of the Met

Avenue 🐚 Aquarium 718/265-3474 🕙 Aquarium daily 10–5, summer weekends and holidays 10–7 🍴 Cafés 🚇 D, F, N, Q Coney Island–Stillwell Avenue 💲 Aquarium moderate, Luna Park expensive

FLUSHING MEADOWS–CORONA PARK

The attractions here are the New York Hall of Science and Queens Museum of Art. The former is a hands-on science and technology museum with a great Science Playground for kids (111th Street; tel 718/699-0005, www.nysci.org). The Queens Museum of Art (New York Building; tel 718/592-9700, www.queensmuseum.org) holds a scale panorama of New York. Outside stands the Unisphere— the world's largest globe. In late summer, the US Open tennis tournament is played in Arthur Ashe Stadium.
➕ See map ▷ 111

HARLEM

The capital of black culture in America during the Harlem Renaissance in the 1920s, the neighborhood is going through a 21st-century rebirth, with skyrocketing real estate prices. Music lovers should check out the Apollo Theater (253 W 125th Street, tel 212/531-5300) for big-name acts or the famous amateur showcase. Nearby, the Studio Museum in Harlem (144 W 125th Street, tel 212/864-4500) displays contemporary art and retrospectives. Historic exhibits are mounted at the Schomburg Center for Research in Black Culture (515 Malcolm X Boulevard, tel 917/275-6975).
➕ See map ▷ 110

STATEN ISLAND

There are several historic sights here. Alice Austen House (2 Hylan Boulevard, tel 718/816-4506, www.aliceausten.org) is a museum of photographs by Alice Austen in her colonial home. Historic Richmond Town (441 Clarke Avenue, tel 718/351-1611, www.historicrichmondtown.org) recreates daily life in a 19th-century village.
➕ See map ▷ 110

YANKEE STADIUM

www.yankees.mlb.com
The Yankees dominated the early era of baseball. In 1920, Babe Ruth joined the team and quickly became a hero. The team clinched the World Series title in 1996, 1998, 1999, 2000 and 2009, the year they moved into their new Yankee Stadium.
➕ See map ▷ 111 ✉ E 161st Street, Bronx 🐚 718/293-4300 🕙 Season runs Apr–Oct. Check schedule for games 🍴 Concession stands 🚇 4, B, D 161st Street/Yankee Stadium 💲 Expensive

The Yankee Stadium in the Bronx, home of the New York Yankees

City Tours

This section contains self-guided tours that will help you explore the sights in each of the city's regions. Each tour is designed to take a day, with a map pinpointing the recommended places along the way. There is a quick reference guide at the end of each tour, listing everything you need in that region, so you know exactly what's close by.

Lower Manhattan

The cradle of New York, Lower Manhattan is steeped in history—new immigrants landed here from the 17th century until the early 20th century—as well as the Financial District, historic Seaport and fashionable SoHo.

Morning
Start the day at the tip of Manhattan in **Battery Park** (▷ 66), with its splendid views of New York Harbor. Ferries for the **Statue of Liberty** (▷ 54–55) and **Ellis Island** (▷ 26–27) leave from Castle Clinton, but save these for a separate day. Cross State Street to admire the beautiful Beaux Arts facade of the **U.S. Custom House** (▷ 73), housing the National Museum of the American Indian. Then proceed along Bowling Green, the small square opposite, past the Charging Bull statue (right), a symbol of Wall Street.

Mid-morning
Walk up Broadway and note the plaques for over a century of ticker tape parades. Continue north to visit the **World Trade Center**. Farther south, **Trinity Church** (left; ▷ 59) marks the west end of **Wall Street** (▷ 58–59); stroll around the old churchyard, then head down Wall Street to **Federal Hall**, the **New York Stock Exchange** and other sites.

Lunch
Rub shoulders with Financial District workers and have a pub lunch at **The Bailey Pub & Brasserie** (▷ 142), one block north of Wall Street. The steak frites is delicious, or try a hearty *plat du jour* such as shepherd's pie.

Afternoon
Walk north on Front Street to **South Street Seaport** (▷ 72). From the waterfront along the East River there are good views of **Brooklyn Bridge** (▷ 66). Follow Dover Street west to **City Hall** (▷ 67), then take Centre Street north into **Chinatown** (▷ 20–21). Explore its bustling markets, its quiet temples and herbalist shops. If you're baffled by the many shops selling Chinese wares, **Pearl River Mart** (▷ 122) has everything you could wish for under one roof.

Mid-afternoon
Chinatown spills north into **Little Italy**. Walk north on Mulberry Street, past the **Italian American Museum** (▷ 68), and when you reach **St. Patrick's Old Cathedral** (▷ 72), turn left on Prince Street, which will bring you into **SoHo** (▷ 52–53). Grab a coffee at **Dean & DeLuca** (▷ 52) to keep you going as you browse the art galleries, ogle the cast-iron buildings and indulge in some shopping. Most stores here stay open into early evening.

Evening
There are plenty of ultra-chic bars in SoHo for a cocktail or a nightcap. For some old SoHo atmosphere, try **Fanelli's** (94 Prince Street, between Mercer and Greene streets, tel 212/226-9412).

Dinner
After drinks, make your way east to **Delicatessen** (▷ 144), where they serve updated versions of classic comfort food. There's great SoHo people-watching from its outdoor tables. If you want something even more old-school, make **Lombardi's** (32 Spring Street at Mott Street, tel 212/941-7994) your destination. It was the first sit-down pizzeria in America.

East 1st Street

EAST HOUSTON STREET

Hamilton
Fish Park

Eldridge Street
Ludlow Street
Essex Street
Norfolk Street
Suffolk Street
Clinton Street
Attorney Street
Ridge Street
Pitt Street
Columbia Street
FDR DRIVE

Stanton Street

Stanton Street
ALLEN STREET
Orchard Street
Rivington Street

WILLIAMSBURG BRIDGE

DELANCEY STREET
Delancey Street
Essex Street
Suffolk Street
Clinton Street
Sheriff Street
Pitt Street
Broome Street
Lewis Street
FDR Drive

Delancey Street

Lower East Side Tenement Museum

NORFOLK ST

GRAND STREET

Eldridge Street
Allen Street
Grand Street
Forsyth Street
Hester Street

LOWER EAST SIDE

Seward Park

East Broadway

Henry Street
Madison Street
Jackson Street
Gouverneur Street
Cherry Street

Corlears Hook Park

Canal Street

East Broadway

Jefferson Street
Clinton Street
Montgomery Street
Water Street
Front Street

Pier 42 Park

Eldridge Street Synagogue

Forsyth St

Broadway
Henry Street
Rutgers Street
Jefferson Street

Cherry Street

SOUTH STREET

Schaefer Landing / S Williamsburg

Division Street
East Broadway
Market Street
Pike Street

FRANKLIN D ROOSEVELT (FDR) DRIVE

THE BOWERY

Canal Street

Henry Street
Market Street
Catherine Street
Monroe Street

East River

Catherine Street
Madison Street
Monroe Street
Cherry Street

Water Street

Pike Slip

Market Slip

Catherine Slip

MANHATTAN BRIDGE

CITY TOURS

Robert F Wagner Snr Pl

VINEGAR HILL

John Street
Plymouth Street
Water Street
Front Street
York Street
Jay Street
Bridge Street
Gold Street
John St

Dover Street

Pike Slip

Rock Slip

Fulton Street Market

Brooklyn Bridge

BROOKLYN BRIDGE

ROOSEVELT (FDR) DRIVE

Brooklyn Bridge Park

Empire-Fulton Ferry State Park

DUMBO

Adams Street
Washington Street
Main Street
Front Street
Water Street

York Street

278

South Street Seaport

Brooklyn Bridge Park / DUMBO

Old Fulton Street

Doughty Street

FULTON FERRY

York St

Furman Street

Poplar Street

Middagh Street

Cranberry Street

Orange Street

Pineapple Street

Henry Street
Hicks Street
Willow Street

Columbia Heights

Clark Street

Monroe Place

High Street

Cadman Plaza Park

Courthouse

Adams Street
Jay Street

TILLARY STREET

Post Office

Johnson Street

NY State Supreme Court

Pier 11 Wall Street Terminal

Brooklyn Bridge Park

BROOKLYN-QUEENS EXPRESSWAY

BROOKLYN HEIGHTS

Love Lane

Pierrepont Street

Montague Street

Remsen Street

Grace Court

CADMAN PLAZA WEST

Clark Street

Brooklyn Historical Society

Montague Ter

Hicks Street

Henry Street

Grace Ct Alley

Hunts La

Clinton Street

Court Street

Brooklyn Borough Hall

Court St

BROOKLYN

0   500 m

0   500 yds

Paulus Hook

Belford / Harbor Way

Governors Island

G   H   J

81

Lower Manhattan Quick Reference Guide

TOP 25 SIGHTS AND EXPERIENCES

Chinatown (▷ 20)
Explore this bustling neighborhood of street-side produce stalls, herbalist shops, Buddhist temples, dim sum parlors and tempting restaurants.

Ellis Island (▷ 26)
Follow in the footsteps of millions of immigrants, most of whom traveled in cramped steerage class, who passed through this gateway to New York and the New World.

SoHo (▷ 52)
SoHo features leading art galleries, trendy boutiques, top fashion chains, cool bars and chic restaurants in 19th-century cast-iron buildings.

Statue of Liberty (▷ 54)
A visit to this iconic landmark is a must on any visit to New York. The ferry ride to the island is impressive, and the view from the statue's crown is breathtaking.

Wall Street (▷ 58)
During Dutch colonial times, Wall Street marked the northern boundary of New York. Now home to bankers and brokers it's the powerhouse of the US economy.

World Trade Center (▷ 62)
The National September 11 Memorial, on the site of the Twin Towers, is both impressive and poignant. It's a quiet place for peace and contemplation.

Downtown and Chelsea

The area from Houston Street north to 30th Street encompasses NoHo and the East Village, the tree-lined streets of Greenwich Village, the Meatpacking District with its trendy stores and clubs, and Chelsea, home of the High Line and the Whitney Museum of American Art

Morning

Start the day with breakfast at one of the bakeries in **Chelsea Market** (right; ▷ 121). You can either eat there or take it with you up to the **High Line** (▷ 40). Begin your explorations on this converted railbed by heading north, but eventually wend your way to the Gansevoort Street end of the park and the **Whitney Museum of American Art** (▷ 60).

Late morning/lunch

Leave the High Line at its southern terminus and strike our for the heart of the Village along Bleecker Street. If you need a snack, you'll pass **Magnolia Bakery** (401 Bleecker Street), made (in) famous by the film *Sex and the City*. When Bleecker Street reaches MacDougal Street, head north. These blocks were the epicenter of the early '60s folk scene. You'll soon reach **Washington Square** (▷ 73) which is a great place for people-watching. But first, lunch! The bistro-style **North Square Restaurant** (▷ 147) in the **Washington Square Hotel** (▷ 159) is a good choice for Mediterranean dishes.

Afternoon

After lunch, stroll through Washington Square to its southern side (West 4th Street) and begin walking east to the **East Village** (▷ 24–25). **The Merchant's House Museum** is a fascinating look back at an earlier era, complete with furnishings that were moved into the house in the 1830s. Then make your way up to **St. Mark's Place** (E 8th Street) with its funky mix of ethnic restaurants and shops.

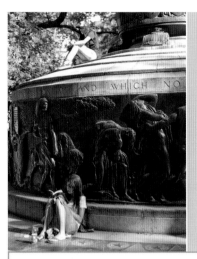

Late afternoon

From the East Village head back to Broadway and the **Strand Bookstore** (▷ 125) and **Grace Church** (▷ 68) which has free audio tours via mobile phone. Just a few blocks north of the church is **Union Square** (left, ▷ 73). Visit on a Monday, Wednesday, Friday or Saturday, and you'll be able to browse the food stands of **Union Square Greenmarket** (▷ 125).

Evening

For a historic watering hole, head for the **White Horse Tavern** (▷ 137) on Hudson Street, where poet Dylan Thomas drank his last. Or head up to 23rd Street: At Fifth Avenue is **Eataly** (▷ 121), which has imported Italian goods and several fine restaurants. Further west is the **Chelsea Hotel** (▷ 66), favored by the Dylans (Bob and Thomas).

Dinner

If you're not dining at Eataly, return to the **Meatpacking District** (below right; ▷ 69) for **Fatty Crab** (▷ 145), where high-end cocktails meet riffs on Malaysian street food.

Late evening

After dinner, you are spoiled for choice. Stay in the Meatpacking District or head back to the West Village for cool jazz at the **Blue Note** (▷ 132) or the **Village Vanguard** (178 7th Avenue South at W 11th Street, tel 212/255-4037). The clubs on Bleecker and MacDougal Street feature live music, too, with **Le Poisson Rouge** (158 Bleecker, tel 212/505-3474) and **SubCulture** (45 Bleecker, tel 212/533-5470) drawing a wide and interesting range of acts.

Midtown W 17th St
LINCOLN TUNNEL 495
Pier 76
Jacob Javits Convention Center

West 39th Street
West 38th Street
West 37th Street
West 36th Street
West 35th Street
34th Street Penn Station
WEST 34TH STREET
West 33rd Street

GARMENT DISTRICT

Macy's
34th Street Penn Station
34th Street Herald Square

HUDSON YARDS

Area under redevelopment

West 31st Street

Madison Square Garden
PENN STATION

WEST 30TH STREET
West 30th Street

West 29th Street
West 28th Street
Chelsea Park
West 27th Street
West 26th Street
West 25th Street
West 24th Street
West 23rd Street
West 22nd Street
West 21st Street

28th Street

MANHATTAN

CHELSEA

23rd Street   23rd Street   West 23rd St
23rd Street

Chelsea Hotel

West 20th Street
West 19th Street
West 18th Street
West 17th Street
West 16th Street
West 15th Street

Rubin Museum of Art

18th Street

Chelsea Piers

Chelsea Market

MEATPACKING DISTRICT

WEST 14TH STREET

14th Street   14th Street   14th Street

8th Avenue   6th Avenue

West 13th Street
Little West 12th Street

Fatty Crab

WEST VILLAGE

Whitney Museum of American Art

Gansevoort St
Horatio Street
Jane Street
Bethune Street
Bank Street

Magnolia Bakery

White Horse Tavern

Village Vanguard

Waverly

Christopher Street Sheridan Square
West Washington Place

GREENWICH VILLAGE

Hudson River

Barrow Street
Morton Street
Leroy Street
Clarkson Street

West Houston Street

Houston Street

Children's Museum of the Arts

New York City Fire Department Museum

King

Pier 40

High Line

Chelsea Waterside Park

West 30th Street Heliport

West 39th Street | West 39th | Street
West 38th Street | East 38th Street
West 37th Street | East 37th Street
KOREATOWN | **Morgan Library & Museum**
West 36th Street | East 36th Street
West 35th Street | East 35th Street | E 34th St/Midtown
W 34TH STREET | EAST 34TH STREET | EAST 34TH STREET | East 34th Street Heliport
Empire State Building
West 33rd Street | East 33rd Street | East 33rd Street
West 32nd Street | East 32nd Street | 33rd Street | East 32nd Street
MIDTOWN SOUTH
West 31st Street | East 31st Street | East 31st Street | **KIPS BAY**
West 30th Street | East 30th Street | East 30th Street
West 29th Street | East 29th Street | East 29th Street
W 28th Street | 28th Street
28th Street | East 28th Street | East 28th Street
West 27th St | East 27th Street | East 27th Street
West 26th St | East 26th Street | East 26th Street
West 25th St | East 25th Street | East 25th Street
Madison Square Park
West 24th Street | East 24th Street | East 24th Street
FLATIRON DISTRICT
23rd Street | East 23rd Street | 23rd Street | East 23rd Street
Eataly | **Flatiron Building**
West 22nd Street | 22nd Street | East 22nd Street
West 21st Street | East 21st Street | East 21st Street
Theodore Roosevelt Birthplace | **Gramercy Park** | **GRAMERCY**
West 20th Street | East 20th Street | East 20th Street
West 19th Street | **Block Beautiful** | East 19th Street | East 19th Street
West 18th Street | East 18th Street | East 18th Street
West 17th Street | East 17th Street | East 17th Street | **STUYVESANT TOWN**
Union Square
West 16th Street | East 16th Street | **Stuyvesant Square** | East 16th St
UNION SQUARE
West 15th Street | East 15th Street | East 15th St
Union Square Park
WEST 14TH ST | EAST 14TH STREET | 3rd Avenue | EAST 14TH STREET | 1st Avenue
14th Street-Union Square
West 13th Street | East 13th Street | East 13th Street
Strand Bookstore
West 12th Street | East 12th Street | East 12th Street
West 11th Street | East 11th Street | East 11th Street
Grace Church
West 10th Street | East 10th Street | East 10th Street | **EAST VILLAGE AND NOHO**
West 9th Street | East 9th Street | East 9th Street | **Tompkins Square Park**
8th Street-NYU
North Square Restaurant | East 8th Street | St Marks Place
Washington Square | Astor Place | **ALPHABET CITY**
Waverly Place | East 7th Street
Washington Square North | East 6th Street
Washington Square Park | Washington Place | East 5th Street
Washington Square South | **The Ukranian Museum** | East 4th Street
West 4th Street | **Merchant's House Museum** | East 3rd Street
West Washington Sq
Blue Note | West 3rd Street | Great Jones Street | East 2nd Street
Bond Street | East 1st Street
Bleecker Street | Bleecker Street | EAST HOUSTON STREET
Le Poisson Rouge | **Subculture** | **NOLITA**
WEST HOUSTON STREET
St Patrick's Old Cathedral
Prince Street | **New Museum of Contemporary Art**
Prince Street | Stanton Street
E | **F** | **Lower East Side Tenement Museum** | **G**
Spring Street | Spring Street
SOHO | Bowery

Downtown and Chelsea
Quick Reference Guide

CITY TOURS

East Village and NoHo (▷ 24)
The East Village, with immigrant history and counterculture vibe, is well worth exploring. Nearby NoHo, once one of the most elegant residential neighborhoods in the city, still features beautiful homes and cobblestone streets.

Greenwich Village (▷ 36)
Once an actual village, this area has gorgeous, tree-lined streets. It was the center of the folk revival of the 1960s, birthplace of the gay rights movement, and has been home to generations of artists and writers.

High Line (▷ 40)
Local residents banded together to turn this abandoned elevated railbed into one of New York's premier parks. The park has attracted shops, restaurants, and high-end apartment construction, while still retaining its charm.

Whitney Museum of American Art (▷ 60)
One of the finest collections of 20th-century American art, the Whitney has expanded its scope with a move from the Upper East Side to the Meatpacking District while still showcasing the permanent collection that made it famous.

Midtown

Midtown is a must for visitors. It has leading museums, pulsating Times Square, Grand Central Terminal plus the magnet for shoppers—Fifth Avenue. It also has three of New York's most famous skyscrapers, two with observatories for stupendous views.

Morning
Get an early start at **Rockefeller Center** (▷ 50–51). The subway concourse below the GE Building and surrounding the plaza is full of restaurants; pick up a coffee and breakfast sandwich at **'wichcraft**, or have a more substantial breakfast at the **Rock Center Cafe**, which looks out on the famous ice rink. Be sure to see the many beautiful artworks around the complex, before or after enjoying the observation decks at **Top of the Rock** (right) for majestic city views.

Mid-morning
Walk west along 50th Street to **Radio City Music Hall** (▷ 136), and turn right up Sixth Avenue. Turn right on 53rd Street to visit the **Museum of Modern Art** (▷ 46–47).

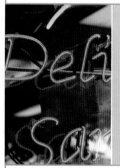

Lunch
"Quick" and "inexpensive" are foreign words in this part of Midtown. Your best bet for a simple lunch that won't break the bank is to grab a bite at one of MoMA's cafés. Or if you're dying for a delicious deli sandwich, one of New York's most famous eateries is nearby, the **Carnegie Deli** (854 7th Avenue at 55th Street). You can't go wrong with their pastrami and corned beef on rye.

Afternoon
Walk east to **Fifth Avenue** (▷ 30–31) and let the shopping spree begin—even if you're just window shopping and ogling the fabulous displays. If you enter only one store, make it **Saks Fifth Avenue** (▷ 125); the perfume and cosmetic counters fill the ground floor. Just north is the beautiful **St. Patrick's Cathedral** (▷ 71).

Mid-afternoon
Turn east on 45th Street and walk to the Park Avenue entrance of **Grand Central Terminal** (▷ 34–35). Admire its stunning main concourse, then head downstairs for a welcome rest and a snack in the **Dining Concourse** (▷ 145). Exit on 42nd Street, and detour one block east to step into the art deco lobby of the **Chrysler Building** (▷ 67). Then walk west on 42nd Street to Fifth Avenue, and visit the **New York Public Library** (left; ▷ 48–49).

Evening
As dusk falls, continue west and turn right up Broadway into **Times Square** (▷ 56–57), in all its neon glory. Head for the **TKTS booth** (▷ 56), where you may get a discount ticket for a Broadway show.

Dinner
Times Square is notorious for chain restaurants, but a good choice for real New York fare is **John's Pizzeria** (▷ 146). There's a branch of **Carmine's** (▷ 144) at 200 W 44th Street, off Times Square.

Late evening
Afterwards, take in that Broadway show, and/or grab a cab to end the evening with the best nightcap of all: the view of the twinkling lights of Manhattan from the top of the **Empire State Building** (right; ▷ 28–29).

East 60th Street
Lexington Avenue/ 59th Street
59th Street
East 60th Street

EAST 59TH STREET
SUTTON PLACE
East 59th Street
East 58th Street
East 58th Street

SUTTON PL

EAST 57TH STREET
EAST 57TH STREET

East 56th Street
East 56th Street

Sutton Place South

East 55th Street
East 55th Street

MIDTOWN EAST
East 54th Street
East 54th Street

Lexington Avenue/ 53rd Street
Lipstick Building
East 53rd Street
East 53rd Street

Seagram Building
TURTLE BAY
East 52nd St
East 52nd Street

51st Street
East 51st St
East 51st Street

Park Avenue
Lexington Avenue
3RD AVENUE
2ND AVENUE
1ST AVENUE

E 50th St
East 50th Street
Mitchell Pl
Beekman Pl

E 49th St
East 49th Street

E 48th St
East 48th Street

Madison Avenue

E 47th Street
East 47th Street

East 46th Street
East 46th Street

United Nations Headquarters
East 45th Street
East 45th Street

Grand Central Terminal
East River
E 44th St
East 44th Street

E 43rd St
TUDOR CITY
East 43rd Street

Chrysler Building
EAST 42ND ST
EAST 42ND STREET

Grand Central 42nd Street
Daily News Building
Chanin Building
East 41st Street
East 41st Street

MURRAY HILL
East 40th Street
East 40th Street

Madison Avenue
Park Avenue
Lexington Avenue
3RD AVENUE
2ND AVENUE
1ST AVENUE

FRANKLIN D ROOSEVELT (FDR) DRIVE

E 39th St
East 39th Street

E 38th St
East 38th Street

E 37th St
Morgan Library & Museum
East 36th Street

E 34th St/ Midtown

East 35th Street
East 35th Street

EAST 34TH STREET
EAST 34TH STREET

East 34th Street Heliport

East 33rd St
33rd Street
East 33rd Street

Park Avenue S

East 32nd St
500 m
500 yds

East 31st St
KIPS BAY
East 30th Street

E
F
G

N

CITY TOURS

93

Midtown Quick Reference Guide

Empire State Building (▷ 28)
The most famous New York sky-scraper affords panoramic views over Manhattan by day or night.

Fifth Avenue (▷ 30)
For high fashion, style and quality, there's no better place to shop than Fifth Avenue.

Grand Central Terminal (▷ 34)
Some half a million people pass through this stunning Beaux Arts concourse every day.

Museum of Modern Art (▷ 46)
From 19th-century masterpieces to contemporary art, this is one of the city's leading museums.

New York Public Library (▷ 48)
See the fine carved ceiling and the glorious reading rooms of this Beaux Arts landmark.

Rockefeller Center (▷ 50)
Admire the plaza and artworks of this urban complex, then take in the view from the Top of the Rock.

Times Square (▷ 56)
Come here at night to see the blitz of neon at the heart of New York's famous Theater District or browse in its megastores by day.

CITY TOURS

Upper East Side and Central Park

Central Park is a huge green space accessible to all New Yorkers. The museums of the Upper East Side, facing the park along Fifth Avenue, are renowned worldwide. Their collections range from priceless antiquities to modern art, design, ethnic culture and history.

Morning

It's unlikely you'll visit more than two museums in a day. This tour will take you past the most popular, and give you a taste of Central Park in between. Most museums don't open until 10am, so start with an early morning stroll in **Central Park** (left; ▷ 18–19). Enter at the south-east corner by Grand Army Plaza (E 59th Street and 5th Avenue). A pedestrian path (just in from 5th Avenue) leads to the zoo. If you follow the paved road, first detour to the Pond, with lovely views of the skyline, before reaching the Dairy Visitor Center, where you can pick up a park map. Continue north along The Mall, lined with one of the largest stands of elm trees in America. The southern end, Literary Walk, has statues of famous writers.

Mid-morning

Just before the Naumburg Bandshell, veer right and follow paths to exit the park at 69th Street. Go one block north to visit the **Frick Collection** (▷ 32–33). Otherwise, continue through the park to the Bethesda Terrace and Fountain (right), overlooking the Lake. Admire the view, then take the pedestrian walkway beneath the terrace—look up to see the Minton tile ceiling, designed by British architect Jacob Wrey Mould. Follow the lakeside path to your right. At Loeb Boathouse veer right to the Conservatory Water, the pretty model boat pond.

Lunch

The Met, Guggenheim, Cooper-Hewitt and Neue Galerie
all have cafés. In Central Park, the **Loeb Boathouse** restaurant
(▷ 147) has an express café as well as formal dining on the terrace.
Alternatively picnic on the Great Lawn behind the Met.

Afternoon

A visit to the **Metropolitan
Museum of Art** (left; ▷ 44–45)
is always worthwhile. It stands
right in Central Park. Try to catch
a free tour of the museum's
highlights (times vary). At Fifth
Avenue and 86th Street is the
Neue Galerie (▷ 70). Further
north at 89th Street is the
Guggenheim Museum (▷ 38–
39), housed in Frank Lloyd
Wright's stunning circular
building. Beyond is the **Cooper
Hewitt Smithsonian Design
Museum** (▷ 22–23) and the
Jewish Museum (▷ 68). All of
these face Central Park's famous
Reservoir. The running track and
bridle path around the Reservoir
are good places to stroll.

Evening

In summer, Central Park has evening events (Shakespeare in the Park;
concerts on the Great Lawn), but be aware of your surroundings when
in the park after dark. If a museum has a late night, evenings are a
good time to visit and explore, or head for a cocktail at **Bemelmans
Bar** (Carlyle Hotel, 35 E 76th Street, tel 212/744-1600).

Dinner

The superb cuisine at nearby **Café Boulud** (▷ 143) makes it a good
choice for dinner.

Late evening

Return to Carlyle Hotel's **Café Carlyle** (▷ 132) for jazz and cabaret.

Jewish Museum

Cooper Hewitt Smithsonian Design Museum

Guggenheim Museum

Neue Galerie

Metropolitan Museum of Art

Jacqueline Kennedy Onassis Reservoir

Central Park

Arthur Ross Pinetum

The Great Lawn

86th Street Transverse

Delacorte Theater

Cleopatra's Needle

Turtle Pond

81st Street (Museum of Natural History)

Belvedere Castle

79th Street Transverse

Cedar Hill

American Museum of Natural History

The Ramble

New-York Historical Society

Café Carlyle, Bemelman's Bar

Café Boulud

The San Remo

The Loeb Boathouse

The Dakota

The Lake

Conservatory Water

Cherry Hill

Bethesda Terrace

East Green

Strawberry Fields

72nd Street

72nd Street Transverse

Naumburg Bandshell

Frick Collection

The Mall

Sheep Meadow

Literary Walk

Tavern on the Green

Tisch Children's Zoo

65th Street Transverse

Dairy Visitor Center

Central Park Zoo

Lincoln Center

Heckscher Ballfields

Wollman Skating Rink

Time Warner Center

Coliseum Park

Columbus Circle

59th Street Columbus Circle

The Pond

5th Avenue/ 59th Street

Central Park South

West 58th Street

Central Park Driveway

West Drive

East Drive

Central Park Drive

Central Park West

Columbus Avenue

Broadway

5th Avenue

Madison Avenue

CITY TOURS

Upper East Side and Central Park
Quick Reference Guide

Central Park (▷ 18)

This great, green expanse is a visionary creation in the heart of the city. Join New Yorkers as they walk, jog, cycle, row, picnic, stroll with their dogs, play ball and escape the urban buzz.

Cooper Hewitt Smithsonian Design Museum (▷ 22)

Having reopened following refurbishment, the superb collections of furniture and decorative arts in the Carnegie mansion are stunning.

Frick Collection (▷ 32)

The mansion of this 19th-century robber baron is worth a visit in itself, and forms a splendid backdrop for his magnificent collection of old masters and decorative arts.

Guggenheim Museum (▷ 38)

Frank Lloyd Wright's ground-breaking, nautilus-shaped building with its internal spiral walkway gets all the glory, but the collection of late19th- and 20th-century art is also superb.

Metropolitan Museum of Art (▷ 44)

Don't be daunted by the sheer vastness of this fabulous art museum. Viewing just one or two of its wonderful collections will leave lasting memories.

CITY TOURS

Upper West Side

The area west of Central Park is a largely residential, pleasantly leafy neighborhood of grand apartment buildings and big brownstones. Its major attractions are Lincoln Center and the wonderful American Museum of Natural History.

Morning

Start at **Lincoln Center** (▷ 42–43). Walk around the plaza, admiring the Revson Fountain, the Metropolitan Opera House and other cultural venues. Guided tours are available if you want to go behind the scenes; they leave from the David Rubenstein Atrium. From the northeast corner of the Lincoln Center, cross over the intersection with Broadway to the **American Folk Art Museum** (left; ▷ 66). Continue up Columbus Avenue, taking in its shops and restaurants. If you're ready for a snack, you'll pass the **Magnolia Bakery** (200 Columbus Avenue)—it's never too early for one of their cupcakes.

Mid-morning

Turn right on W 72nd Street. On the corner with Central Park West is the Dakota, the first luxury co-op apartment building on the Upper West Side. Its most famous resident, John Lennon, was fatally shot outside the south gate in 1980. Cross over the road to enter **Central Park** (▷ 18–19), and follow the path to Strawberry Fields, where the black-and-white *Imagine* mosaic (right) is the centerpoint of a peace garden and a memorial to the singer-songwriter. From here there is a good view of the Dakota and the towers of the neighboring San Remo Apartments. Farther on is the **New-York Historical Society** (▷ 71). Cross back to Central Park West and continue on 73rd Street to Broadway.

Lunch

Broadway is another great shopping street. Continue north to 80th Street, where you can put together a picnic from the gourmet fare at **Zabar's** (right; ▷ 125), or get a sandwich at their adjoining café. Take it to **Riverside Park**, two blocks west, with views over the Hudson River.

Afternoon

Plan to spend the entire afternoon at the **American Museum of Natural History** (▷ 14–15). Highlights include the dinosaur halls, are the animal dioramas, the Rose Center for Earth and Space (left) and more.

Dinner

You won't have too much further to walk for an early dinner at **Ouest** (▷ 148). Sink into the red leather booths and enjoy the inspired cuisine of Tom Valenti, one of New York's favorite chefs.

Evening

The No. 1 subway is not far away for a quick ride back to **Lincoln Center** (right). Even if you haven't got tickets for an evening performance, a walk through the lit-up plaza is a magical way to end the day.

Jewish Museum

East 92nd Street

East 91st Street

Cooper Hewitt Smithsonian Design Museum

East 90th Street

Jacqueline Kennedy Onassis Reservoir

East 89th Street

Guggenheim Museum

East 88th Street

East 87th Street

Park Avenue

Lexington Avenue

3RD AVENUE

86th Street

86th Street Transverse

Neue Galerie

East 86th Street

East 85th Street

Central Park

East 84th Street

Arthur Ross Pinetum

The Great Lawn

Metropolitan Museum of Art

East 82nd Street

East Drive

5th Avenue

Delacorte Theater

Cleopatra's Needle

East 81st Street

East 80th Street

Turtle Pond

Belvedere Castle

East 79th Street

79th Street Transverse

Cedar Hill

East 78th Street

The Ramble

East 77th Street

77th Street

East 76th Street

East 75th Street

The Loeb Boathouse

East 74th Street

The Lake

East Drive

East 73rd Street

Conservatory Water

UPPER EAST SIDE

Central Park Driveway

East 72nd Street

Cherry Hill

East Green

East 71st Street

Asia Society and Museum

3RD AVENUE

Strawberry Fields

72nd Street Transverse

Frick Collection

East 70th Street

Naumburg Bandshell

The Mall

East 69th Street

Madison Avenue

Park Avenue

Hunter College

68th Street Hunter College

West Drive

Sheep Meadow

East 68th Street

Lexington Avenue

5th Avenue

East 67th Street

Tavern on the Green

East Drive

Tisch Children's Zoo

East 66th Street

Central Park

East 65th Street

65th Street Transverse

Central Park Zoo

East 64th Street

Heckscher Ballfields

Wollman Skating Rink

East 63rd Street

Lexington Avenue/ 63rd Street

East Drive

East 62nd Street

0 ———— 250 m
0 ———— 250 yds

West Drive

Central Park Drive

East 61st Street

Lexington Avenue/ 59th Street

The Pond

East 60th Street

5th Avenue/ 59th Street

59th Street

Central Park South

D

E

West 58th Street

East 59th Street

F

Heckscher Ballfields

East 58th Street

SIGHTS AND EXPERIENCES

American Museum of Natural History (▷ 14)

This is the largest natural history museum in the world. The lifesize, rearing Barosaurus in the main entrance hall leads to the renowned dinosaur halls, where fossil specimens of some of the earliest dinosaur discoveries are displayed. Add to that a priceless collection of gemstones, animal dioramas, the Rose Center for Earth and Space with its amazing planetarium, and more, and you could easily spend a day here.

Lincoln Center (▷ 42)

New York's premier performing arts complex is a sight to behold, with its gushing fountains and gleaming buildings, the huge arched windows and chandeliers of the Metropolitan Opera House, and the glowing lights reflected in its wide central plaza. In addition to housing the Metropolitan Opera, it is home to the New York Philharmonic, the Juilliard School of Music, the New York City Ballet and many others, and offers a vast array of entertainment.

View of Central Park West, including the Dakota and San Remo apartments

MORE TO SEE 64

American Folk Art Museum
Museum of Arts and Design
New-York Historical Society

SHOP 114

Accessories
Laila Rowe
Beauty
Bluemercury Apothecary & Spa
Books
Barnes and Noble
Clothes
Malia Mills
Steven Alan

Food and Wine
Zabar's
Sports Goods
Patagonia

ENTERTAINMENT 126

Cinema
Lincoln Plaza Cinema
Classical Music
Avery Fisher Hall
Cathedral of St. John
   the Divine
The Metropolitan Opera
Comedy
Stand Up NY

Dance
David H. Koch Theater
Jazz
Dizzy's Club Coca Cola
Smoke
Live Music
Beacon Theatre
Theater/Performance
Symphony Space

EAT 138

Casual
Barney Greengrass
Boat Basin Café
Contemporary
Jean-Georges
Ouest

Picholine
Tolani Wine Restaurant
Italian
Carmine's

CITY TOURS

Farther Afield

New York's outer boroughs are increasingly attractive to those who seek a more relaxed approach to life. Brooklyn (▷ 16–17) especially has plenty to engage visitors. With an early start, you can take in its top sights as well as two classic New York experiences.

Morning

Join the morning bustle of the city's commuters and begin your day at the tip of Manhattan at the Staten Island Ferry Terminal. Of course, you'll be heading in the opposite direction, but no matter. The ferry ride (right) across Upper New York Bay is stunning in both directions, and even better, it's free. If you can, ride on the ferry's outside deck to get a good view of the Statue of Liberty—visible from the right side of the boat on the outward journey—and other sights. The round trip to and from **Staten Island** (▷ 75) takes an hour; when you arrive you can catch the next ferry back to Manhattan.

Mid-morning

Disembark and walk up Broadway to Bowling Green, where you can catch the No. 4 or 5 subway train to the Brooklyn Bridge/City Hall stop. On Park Row, a sidewalk entrance leads up to the wooden walkway of **Brooklyn Bridge** (left; ▷ 66). A walk (or jog) across the bridge is a must, and New Yorkers love it as much as visitors do. It's about a 20-minute walk, though it can take twice as long with stops to admire the views back to the Manhattan skyline.

Lunch

When you come to the end of the bridge, you'll have worked up an appetite, so when you see the DUMBO sign, take the stairwell down to the street and head towards the water. **Grimaldi's** (▷ 145) on Front Street has some of the best pizza in New York. Afterwards, walk along the promenade for splendid vistas across the river to Manhattan.

Afternoon

Walk through the pretty brownstone-lined streets of Brooklyn Heights to the Clark Street subway stop, and take 2 or 3 subway to the Eastern Parkway stop. This eastern side of Prospect Park contains two of Brooklyn's finest attractions: the **Brooklyn Museum of Art** (right; ▷ 16), and **Brooklyn Botanic Garden** (900 Washington Avenue, tel 718/623-7200), with its rose garden, bonsai museum and Japanese Hill-and-Pond Garden. A visit to either could take up the rest of the afternoon.

Dinner

To get to Williamsburg and **Peter Luger** (▷ 148) for dinner, the quickest route is to take the 2 or 3 subway to Fulton Street in Manhattan and change to the J train to Marcy Ave. If pricey red meat isn't your thing, stroll along Bedford Avenue, which is lined with inexpensive dining options.

Late evening

Williamsburg is filled with fun bars and live music. A good bet is the **Music Hall of Williamsburg** (66 N Sixth Street, tel 718/486-5400), which draws local talent, internationally known indie rockers, spoken word artists and more. Or venture into neighboring Greenpoint to the **Black Rabbit** (91 Greenpoint Avenue, tel 718/349-1595), a local watering hole with a friendly vibe.

Farther Afield Quick Reference Guide

TOP 25 SIGHTS AND EXPERIENCES

Brooklyn (▷ 16–17)

If you've ever wondered what New York is like beyond Manhattan, Brooklyn is the best place to start. Brooklyn Heights is lined with classic brownstones. The Brooklyn Museum of Art contains a renowned Egyptian collection and the Sackler Center for Feminist Art. Alongside is the Brooklyn Botanic Garden. Walk back to Manhattan across the Brooklyn Bridge—a classic New York experience. Williamsburg, with its trendy boutiques and bars, is lively on evenings and weekends.

MORE TO SEE — 64

Bronx Zoo
The Cloisters
Coney Island
Flushing Meadows–Corona Park
Harlem
Staten Island
Yankee Stadium

EAT — 138

Casual
Grimaldi's
Classic NY
Peter Luger

Contemporary
Blue Ribbon
Grocery
Henry's End
River Café

CITY TOURS

1920
THE WONDER WHEEL,
A 150 FOOT TALL FERRIS WHEEL
OPENS AT CONEY ISLAND.

Shop

Whether you're looking for the best local products, a department store or a quirky boutique, you'll find them all in New York. In this section shops are listed alphabetically.

SHOP

Introduction

Thought there was nothing you couldn't buy over the Internet? Think again. New York is a shopping heaven, with clothing, furniture, food and souvenirs available no place else. Shopping is still one of the best ways to get an inside look at life in New York—its trends, pace, cultural influences and sense of humor. From massive department stores to small boutiques, the city has something for everyone.

A Piece of New York

You'll find all kinds of NYC paraphernalia—from Statue of Liberty coin banks and taxicab neckties to sweatshirts bearing the New York Police Department initials and Yankee baseball caps. Museum shops sell reproductions, posters, jewelry, stationery and commemorative items.

Fashion

For fashion head for Nolita and SoHo, where small (and often expensive) boutiques line the streets. Major franchises can also be found here, along Broadway, and side streets such as Prince Street, Broome Street and Spring Street. For the most upscale fashion choices, head to Madison Avenue north of 59th Street, where the toniest New York shops all have outposts.

Music

Although the growth of downloads has seen the demise of many of the large music retailers, there is still much to delight the

WINDOW SHOPPING

Start on Lexington between 59th and 60th streets and you'll see the flags outside Bloomingdale's. Walk west to Madison Avenue; between 60th and 61st streets is Barney's, for expensive clothing, jewelry, accessories and beauty products. Walk west along 57th Street, past Chanel and Christian Dior, to Bergdorf Goodman. On Fifth Avenue peer in at Gucci, Tiffany's and Henri Bendel.

Clockwise from top: A store on Fifth Avenue; a T-shirt that says it all; pretzels to go; looking for a bargain at

SHOP

enthusiast. The city's branches of Academy Records boast collections of vintage classical and rock vinyl and used CDs; Bleecker Street Records and House of Oldies are prime browsing spots in Greenwich Village; or check out the Metropolitan Opera Shop (www.metoperashop.org) for something a little more classical. Note: most American DVDs cannot be played on European machines.

Bargains

If you're looking for a bargain, try the popular sample sales, where designer brands are marked down as much as 80 percent. Designer sales are often held at open show-rooms over a few days. Arrive early on the first day of the sale for the best selection, though prices do drop as days go by. To find out about upcoming sample sales pick up *New York* magazine or *Time Out New York*.

A Bite to Eat

NYC is known for noshing: hot dogs, a slice of pizza, a bagel with a schmear, and street food from mobile food vendors. These range from Middle Eastern falafel carts to waffle stands and vegan lunch trucks. A handy guide to locating a gourmet food truck around town is www.twitter.com/nystfood/lists/mobile-munchies, which automatically updates.

FLEA MARKETS

You can find everything from silver and beaded jewelry to clothing, artworks and antiques at the Brooklyn Flea (www.brooklynflea.com), which in warm weather is in Williamsburg and in winter months moves to Crown Heights (check website for details). Uptown, check out the huge GreenFlea market on Sunday (✉ Columbus Avenue between 76th and 77th streets ⏰ 10–5.30). In good weather, weekend street fairs pop up in different neighborhoods. Check www.nyctourist.com/st_fairs_calendar.htm for a comprehensive schedule.

the Brooklyn Flea Market; don't miss the Midtown department stores; a boutique in Greenwich Village

Directory

Lower Manhattan

Books
The Mysterious Bookshop
Clothes
Abercrombie & Fitch
Resurrection
Discount
Century 21
Food and Wine
The Pickle Guys
Homewares
Pearl River Mart (▷ panel, 122)
Shoes
Alife Rivington Club
Stationery
Kate's Paperie

Downtown and Chelsea

Accessories
Village Tannery
Beauty
C.O. Bigelow
Kiehl's
Books
Strand
Clothes
Cynthia Rowley
Hotoveli
Jeffrey New York
Marc Jacobs
Scoop
Discount
DSW
Food and Wine
Chelsea Market
Eataly
Union Square Greenmarket
Homewares
ABC Carpet and Home
Shoes
DSW

Midtown

Clothes
Brooks Brothers
Dolce & Gabbana
Thomas Pink
Department Stores
Bergdorf Goodman
Macy's
Saks Fifth Avenue
Homewares
Michael C. Fina
Shoes
Kenneth Cole
Manolo Blahnik
Sports Goods
Niketown New York
Technology
Apple Store
Toys
FAO Schwarz

Upper East Side and Central Park

Books
Kitchen Arts and Letters
Clothes
Calvin Klein
Ralph Lauren
Department Stores
Barneys
Bloomingdale's

Upper West Side

Accessories
Laila Rowe
Beauty
Bluemercury Apothecary & Spa
Books
Barnes and Noble
Clothes
Malia Mills
Steven Alan
Food and Wine
Zabar's
Sports Goods
Patagonia

Shopping A-Z

ABC CARPET AND HOME
www.abchome.com
Here are seven floors of extremely carefully edited homewares, from four-poster beds to handkerchiefs to artisinal lotions. The shared esthetic mixes mid-19th-century design museum, Venetian palace and deluxe hotel.

➕ E15 ✉ 888 Broadway/E 19th Street
☎ 212/473-3000 🚇 4, 5, 6, N, Q, R 14th Street–Union Square

ABERCROMBIE & FITCH
www.abercrombie.com
Teens and college grads are the core customers at this temple to slouchy American style, famous for its rather racy Bruce Weber-shot catalogs. The clothes, though, are perfect for anyone's weekends and the prices are gentle. There are men's and women's lines.

➕ F21 ✉ 199 Water Street/Fulton Street
☎ 212/809-9000 🚇 2, 3, 4, 5, A, C, J, Z Fulton Street-Broadway-Nassau

ALIFE RIVINGTON CLUB
www.alifenewyork.com
Here, behind an unmarked door, sneakers are high fashion, with all the latest footwear from American, European and Japanese brands. Great colors and limited editions are available.

➕ G18 ✉ 158 Rivington Street, between Clinton and Suffolk streets
☎ 212/432-7200 🚇 F, J, Z Delancey Street–Essex Street

APPLE STORE
www.apple.com
This 24-hour-a-day, 365-day-a-year showcase store is certain to delight ingrained Mac-geeks as well as those in thrall to Apple's industry-leading design and stylish simplicity. Stores can also be found around the city in the Meatpacking District, SoHo, and the Upper West Side.

➕ E9 ✉ 767 5th Avenue/59th Street
☎ 212/336-1440 🚇 N, R 5th Avenue–59th Street

BARNES AND NOBLE
www.barnesandnoble.com
This is one of the mega book chain's main New York branches. Check the website for upcoming evening readings and regular author book signing events.

➕ B5 ✉ 2289 Broadway/82nd Street
☎ 212/362-8835 🚇 1 79th Street

The iconic 24-hour Apple Store on Fifth Avenue

A New York institution

BARNEYS
www.barneys.com
Many New Yorkers dress virtually exclusively from this high-fashion store. Ranging over several floors are avant-garde designers, the store's own-label clothes, the city's best high-end cosmetics and fragrance departments, a huge range of hip jeans labels, great menswear, an epic shoe department, jewelry, homewares, kids' clothes and more. Prices are high.
➕ E9 ✉ 660 Madison Avenue/61st Street
☎ 212/826-8900 🚇 N, R 5th Avenue–59th Street

BERGDORF GOODMAN
www.bergdorfgoodman.com
For the most sophisticated shopping experience in New York, the eight-floor fashion-for-lunching ladies department store on the site of a Vanderbilt mansion takes the cake.
➕ E9 ✉ 754 5th Avenue/58th Street
☎ 800/558-1855 🚇 N, R 5th Avenue–59th Street

BLOOMINGDALE'S
www.bloomingdales.com
Bloomingdale's opened in 1879 and is one of the most venerable names in Manhattan, yet it keeps up with the latest trends. Great for jewelry and handbags.
➕ F9 ✉ Lexington/59th Street
☎ 212/705-2000 🚇 4, 5, 6, F, N, R 59th Street

BLUEMERCURY APOTHECARY & SPA
www.bluemercury.com
From top brand cosmetics to spa treatments, hair care, famous fragrances and gorgeous candles, Bluemercury is a welcome addition to the Upper West Side retail experience.
➕ B5 ✉ 2305 Broadway/83rd Street
☎ 212/799-0500 🚇 1 to 86th Street

BROOKS BROTHERS
www.brooksbrothers.com
Home of the preppy, Brooks Brothers also caters to anyone, male or female, who wants to look pulled together (though the men's department is far better). Their basics, like boxer shorts and white dress shirts, are exceptional.

THE SHOPS AT COLUMBUS CIRCLE
The closest thing to a mall in Manhattan, The Shops at Columbus Circle in the Time Warner Center has reclaimed Columbus Circle from the traffic. The stores are on the lowest four levels (restaurants above). The *pièce de résistance* is the Whole Foods Market.
➕ C9 ✉ Time Warner Center, Broadway (59th/60th Street) ☎ 212/823-6300, www.shopsatcolumbuscircle.com 🚇 A, B, C, D, 1 59th Street–Columbus Circle

✉ 346 Madison Avenue/44th Street ☎ 212/682-8800 🚇 4, 5, 6, 7, S to Grand Central

CALVIN KLEIN
www.calvinklein.com
The iconic New York designer's flagship store, designed by John Pawson, is as minimal as his clothing, without even racks to spoil the clean lines (you simply point at a display and request your size). His home line is downstairs.
➕ E9 ✉ 654 Madison Avenue/60th Street ☎ 212/292-9000 🚇 N, R 5th Avenue–59th Street

CENTURY 21
www.c21stores.com
Practically a cult, Century 21 sells discounted chic womenswear, especially by European designers.
➕ E21 ✉ 22 Cortlandt Street between Church Street and Broadway ☎ 212/227-9092 🚇 4, 5 Fulton Street

CHELSEA MARKET
www.chelseamarket.com
More than a store, this enormous former Nabisco factory has an array of unique of food boutiques, bakeries, cafés, coffee shops and delis under one roof. Even if you're not hungry, it's enjoyable to stroll through for the architect-honed warehouse and inhale the mouth-watering aromas.
➕ C15 ✉ 75 9th Avenue/15th Street ☎ 212/652-2110 🚇 A, C, E, L 14th Street

C.O. BIGELOW
www.bigelowchemists.com
The oldest apothecary in America (est. 1838) offers a wide range of products for pampering yourself from head to toe. In addition to well-known international brands,

the store also has its own line, which includes everything from lotions to candles.
➕ D16 ✉ 414 Sixth Avenue/9th Street ☎ 212/533-2700 🚇 A, C, E, B, D, F, M West 4th Street

CYNTHIA ROWLEY
www.cynthiarowley.com
Shop here to equip yourself for a night out on the town in adorable, hip dresses and shoes.
➕ C16 ✉ 376 Bleecker Street (between Perry and Charles streets) ☎ 212/242-3803 🚇 1 Christopher Street–Sheridan Square

DOLCE & GABBANA
www.dolcegabbana.com
This is the flagship New York store for cutting-edge styles from fashion's dynamic duo.
➕ E9 ✉ 717 Fifth Avenue/55th Street ☎ 212/897-9653 🚇 N, R Fifth Avenue E, M Fifth Avenue–53rd Street

DSW
www.dsw.com
DSW stands for "Designer Shoe Warehouse," with Prada, Kate Spade, Via Spiga and other designer names at discounted prices. Choose from women's trendy heels and pumps, sandals and beachwear; men's; children's; sports shoes; handbags and more. Other branches in Midtown and the Upper West Side.
➕ E15 ✉ 40 E 14th Street, Union Square South at University Place ☎ 212/674-2146 🚇 L, N, Q, R, 4, 5, 6 Union Square

EATALY
www.eataly.com.nyc
Offering a cornucopia of fresh and packaged Italian foodstuffs from coffee to gelato to housemade pastas, Eataly is as close as one

can come to a real Italian food bazaar. There are also a dozen places to grab a bite.
⊞ D14 ✉ 200 Fifth Avenue/23rd Street ☎ 212/229-2560 🚇 N, R 23rd Street

FAO SCHWARZ
www.fao.com

The near-legendary toy store has lost its iconic clockwork tower but gained a whole new lease on life. There are plenty of areas for kids to experiment with giant toys you have no intention of dragging home. Don't forget to dance on the piano from *Big*.
⊞ E9 ✉ 767 5th Avenue/58th Street ☎ 212/644-9400 🚇 N, R 5th Avenue–59th Street

HOTOVELI
www.hotoveli.com

Chic French and Italian creations dominate in this West Village emporium, which caters for the style-conscious ladies and men.
⊞ C16 ✉ 271 W 4th Street, between Perry and W 11th streets ☎ 212/206-7722 🚇 1 Christopher Street–Sheridan Square

JEFFREY NEW YORK
www.jeffreynewyork.com

One of the coolest places in the Meatpacking District, this compact department store has a resident DJ, a spacious all-white interior and non-pushy assistants. It all makes for a pleasant visit—and an expensive one if you fall for the wares.
⊞ B15 ✉ 449 W 14th Street/9th–10th avenues ☎ 212/206-1272 🚇 A, C , E, L 14th Street

KATE'S PAPERIE
www.katespaperie.com

The choice of beautiful handmade stationery is overwhelming at this SoHo boutique, as well as journals, photo albums and gifts.
⊞ E18 ✉ 188 Lafayette Street/Broome Street ☎ 212/941-9816 🚇 6 Spring Street

KENNETH COLE
www.kennethcole.com

Come here for quality shoes ranging from urban footwear to trendy fashion styles, and simple but stylish clothes for women and men. The store also sells handbags, jewelry, sunglasses and other accessories.
⊞ E11 ✉ 107 E 42nd Street/Park Avenue ☎ 212/949-8079 🚇 4, 5, 6, 7 Grand Central–42nd Street

KIEHL'S
www.kiehls.com

HIgh-end face and body products, made from naturally derived ingredients, are sold in upscale black-and-white packaging. The store has been an East Village fixture since 1851—the pear tree out front commemorates one that was planted by Dutch colonial governor Peter Stuyvesant.
⊞ F15 ✉ 109 3rd Avenue/13th Street ☎ 212/677-3171 🚇 L to 3rd Avenue

PEARL RIVER MART

Shop here for chrome lunch pails with clip-on lids; embroidered silk pajamas and Suzy Wong dresses; bamboo fans and porcelain rice bowls—all the things, in fact, you can get in the smaller Chinatown emporia, but collected under one roof. The food department sells an eclectic range. Prices are very, very low. ⊞ E18 ✉ 477 Broadway (Broome Street) ☎ 212/431-4770, www.pearlriver.com 🚇 N, R Prince Street

KITCHEN ARTS AND LETTERS

www.kitchenartsandletters.com

This is a veritable treasure trove of cookbooks by leading authors including James Beard and Julia Child. You will find many rare and out-of-print titles as well as the very latest cookbook releases.

E4 ☒ 1435 Lexington Avenue, between 93rd and 94th streets ☎ 212/876-5550 ⊛ 6 96th Street

LAILA ROWE

www.lailarowe.com

This is one of a growing chain-ette of accessories stores, crammed with colorful gear. Expect a fun vibe and selections of jewelry at prices that won't break the bank.

C7 ☒ 493 Columbus Avenue/84th Street ☎ 212/724-2680 ⊛ B, C, 1 86th Street

MACY'S

www.macys.com

The sign outside says it's the largest store in the world, and by the time you've walked the vast floors of this huge department store, you'll believe it.

D12 ☒ 151 W 34th Street/Herald Square ☎ 212/695-4400 ⊛ B, D, F, N, R 34th Street

MALIA MILLS

www.maliamills.com

This swimwear emporium is cherished by every woman who fears her reflection. There are mix-and-match pieces made to fit everyone, in super-cool designs.

C7 ☒ 220 Columbus Avenue/70th Street ☎ 212/874-7200 ⊛ 1, 2, 3, B, C 72nd Street

MANOLO BLAHNIK

www.manoloblahnik.com

Come here for beautifully made shoes by one of the world's great shoe designers.

D10 ☒ 31 W 54th Street ☎ 212/582-3007 ⊛ E, M 5th Avenue–53rd Street

MARC JACOBS

www.marcjacobs.com

Fashion's favorite darling, Marc Jacobs put once-Bohemian Bleecker Street on the retail map.

C16 ☒ 403-405 Bleecker Street/W 11th Street ☎ 212/924-0026 ⊛ 1, 2 Christopher Street–Sheridan Square

The largest store in the world

MICHAEL C. FINA

www.michaelcfina.com

This very exclusive purveyor of gifts and tableware is *the* place for wedding lists.

➕ E9 ✉ 500 Park Avenue/E 59th Street ☎ 800/289-3462 🚇 4, 5, 6, 7 Grand Central

THE MYSTERIOUS BOOKSHOP

www.mysteriousbookshop.com

This is a must for mystery lovers. Staff will lead you to new discoveries alongside writers such as Patricia Highsmith and Raymond Chandler. Rare books are available.

➕ E20 ✉ 58 Warren Street between Church Street and West Broadway ☎ 212/587-1011 🚇 1, 2, 3, A, C, E Chambers Street

NIKETOWN NEW YORK

www.nike.com

You can feel like a professional athlete. Expect high-tech videos and multilevel displays in an industrial atmosphere.

➕ D9 ✉ 6 E 57th Street, between 5th and Madison avenues ☎ 212/891-6453 🚇 N, R 57th Street

For great designer vintage head for Resurrection on Mott Street

PATAGONIA

www.patagonia.com

If you like environmental consciousness with your outdoor wear but still want to look slick while climbing the mountain, or just look like you might have done so, this is your place.

➕ C6 ✉ 426 Columbus Avenue/81st Street ☎ 917/441-0011 🚇 B, C 81st Street–Museum of Natural History

THE PICKLE GUYS

www.thepickleguys.com

Carrying on a Lower East Side tradition, the Pickle Guys still brine the old-fashioned way, selling pickles, olives, pickled watermelon (in season) and more out of barrels in their small storefront much as it might have been done a century ago.

➕ G19 ✉ 49 Essex Street/Grand Street ☎ 212/656-9739 🚇 F Delancey Street, J, Z Essex Street

RALPH LAUREN

www.ralphlauren.com

Distinguished cowboy and English country heritage looks are sold out of the Rhinelander Mansion, a turn-of-the-20th-century house.

➕ E7 ✉ 867 Madison Avenue, between E 71st and 72nd streets ☎ 212/606-2100 🚇 6 68th Street–Hunter College

RESURRECTION

www.resurrectionvintage.com

You'll find a haul of pricey but perfect vintage, with an emphasis on collectible labels: Pucci, Halston, Courrèges, Dior. The owners offer their own line of skirts and tops.

➕ F18 ✉ 217 Mott Street, between Spring and Prince streets ☎ 212/625-1374 🚇 6 Spring Street

SAKS FIFTH AVENUE

www.saksfifthavenue.com

Found on the famous street with the same name, this is the flagship store of the now nationwide chain, with a fabulous range of designer fashions for men and women.

E10 ✉ 611 5th Avenue/49th–50th streets ☎ 212/753-4000 🚇 E, F 5th Avenue

SCOOP

www.scoopnyc.com

Well-known designers (Helmut Lang, Zac Posen) sit alongside Scoop's in-house brand.

B15 ✉ 430 W 14th Street/Washington Street ☎ 212/691-1905 🚇 A, C, E 14th Street

STEVEN ALAN

www.stevenalan.com

A Lower East Side look on the Upper West Side, this is a carefully edited array of cutting-edge labels, some of them available nowhere else—including Alan's own designs.

B5 ✉ 465 Amsterdam Avenue/82nd Street ☎ 212/595-8451 🚇 1, 2, 3, 79th Street–Broadway; A, C, E 81st Street–Central Park West

STRAND

www.strandbooks.com

Filled with 18 miles of new and used books, this fabulous book-store is a New York City institution. From popular and hot-off-the-presses bestsellers to antique volumes purchased from estate sales, the Strand has something for everyone. The New York City section is particularly strong.

E16 ✉ 828 Broadway/12th Street ☎ 212/473-1452 🚇 4, 5, 6, N, Q, R, L to 14th Street–Union Square

THOMAS PINK

www.thomaspink.com

Beautifully tailored shirts for men and women line the shelves of the New York outlet of this classic British label.

E10 ✉ 520 Madison Avenue/E 53rd Street ☎ 212/838-1928 🚇 E, M Fifth Avenue–53rd Street

VILLAGE TANNERY

www.villagetannery.com

Love leather? Look no further—stylish leather goods, designed by artisan Sevestet, made to order and handcrafted from the finest materials can all be found here. There are handbags, briefcases, backpacks, belts and more to choose from.

D17 ✉ 173 Bleecker Street ☎ 212/673-5444 🚇 A, C, E, B, D, F, M West 4th Street–Washington Square

ZABAR'S

www.zabars.com

This foodie haven has a Jewish soul all its own. Cheese, coffee, smoked fish and the like are downstairs, while upstairs show-cases the city's best buys in kitchenwares.

B6 ✉ 2245 Broadway/80th Street ☎ 212/787-2000 🚇 1 79th Street

SHOP

Entertainment

Once you've done with sightseeing for the day, you'll find lots of other great things to do with your time in this chapter, even if all you want to do is relax with a drink. In this section establishments are listed alphabetically.

ENTERTAINMENT

Introduction

As the sun sets over New York, the city becomes a sultry, romantic and mysterious place. For spectacular sunset views, stroll along the pedestrian path on the banks of the Hudson River on the West Side, then wander through Times Square as the bright billboards pop out from the dark sky.

Nightlife

As young New Yorkers explore new frontiers in the city, the Meatpacking District—once known for drugs and prostitution—has become home to trendy bars and clubs. Celebrity sightings are common at Spice Market (403 W 13th Street, tel 212/675-2322) and Cielo (18 Little West 12th Street, tel 212/645-5700). At the other end of the spectrum are biker bars like Hogs & Heifers Saloon (859 Washington Street at W 13th Street, tel 212/929-0655) and Fat Cat Billiards (75 Christopher Street in West Village, tel 212/675-6056), friendly dives where the beer flows cheaply and the music is loud.

A short stroll away, a string of music bars sit cheek by jowl along two blocks of Bleecker Street between La Guardia Place and Sullivan Street, including the venerable folk-rock haven, The Bitter End (147 Bleecker Street, tel 212/673-7030), still going strong after more than 50 years. Around the corner is Café Wha? (▷ 133), where Dylan and Hendrix once played, and now a dance club.

FOR A LAUGH

Comedy clubs are a great way to sample New York's sense of humor. Venues such as Caroline's (✉ 1626 Broadway, at 50th Street ☎ 212/757-4100, www.carolines.com), Upright Citizens Brigade Theatre (✉ 307 W 26th Street, between 8th and 9th ☎ 212/366-9176, www.ucbtheatre.com), Stand Up NY (▷ 137) and Gotham (▷ 134) are popular. At many clubs, you'll see a mix of established acts and rising stars.

Clockwise from top: Blue Note in Greenwich Village is one of the best places for jazz; the old Paramount Theater, Times Square; Alice Tully Hall, Lincoln Center;

Another hot nightlife neighborhood is the Lower East Side, where there's a raft of rock 'n' roll bars fanning out from Ludlow and Stanton streets. Leading the pack are Arlene's Grocery (▷ 131), Pianos (158 Ludlow Street, tel 212/505-3733) and Rockwood Music Hall (196 Allen Street, tel 212/477-2155).

Broadway and Beyond
Top Broadway shows can be expensive, but you can pick up some great bargains at the TKTS booth in Times Square and other locations (www.tdf.org/tkts). Off-Broadway venues are less expensive and you might just catch the next big hit on its way up. A night at Lincoln Center (▷ 42–43) is an unforgettable New York experience, whether you opt for a production at the Metropolitan Opera (▷ 135), a symphony at David Geffen Hall (▷ 131), a ballet at the David H. Koch Theater, or one of the more intimate venues.

Take to the Water
Circle Line Cruises' evening boat rides around Manhattan are a relaxing and memorable way to experience the world's most famous skyline. Board at Pier 83, at 42nd Street on the Hudson River (tel 212/563-3200). Tour guides on board relate the legends of the city (www.circleline42.com).

LIVE MUSIC

Rock bands perform at Bowery Ballroom (✉ 6 Delancey Street, www.boweryballroom.com) and Irving Plaza (✉ 17 Irving Plaza, www.irvingplaza.com), while Madison Square Garden (▷ 134) hosts blockbuster tours. You can hear everything from classical music to pop at Carnegie Hall (▷ 132). Among the top jazz clubs are Blue Note (▷ 132) in Greenwich Village, Iridium (✉ 1650 Broadway, www.theiridium.com) and Village Vanguard (✉ 178 7th Avenue South, www.villagevanguard.com).

Gotham Comedy Club; a quiet table à deux in the Meatpacking District; take to the water to see the New York skyline by night

Directory

ENTERTAINMENT

Lower Manhattan

Bars
Barramundi
The Dead Rabbit Grocery and Grog
Parkside Lounge
The Porterhouse at Fraunces Tavern
Cinema
Film Forum
Clubs
Arlene's Grocery
Beach at Governors Island
S.O.B.'s
Comedy
Comedy Cellar
Live Music
City Winery

Downtown and Chelsea

Bars
McSorley's Old Ale House
Pete's Tavern
White Horse Tavern
Cabaret
Duplex (▷ panel, 134)
Joe's Pub
Clubs
Café Wha?
Comedy
Gotham Comedy Club
Jazz
Blue Note
Karaoke
Sing Sing Karaoke
Live Music
Mercury Lounge
Theater/Performance
Cherry Lane Theatre

Midtown

Bars
Four Seasons Hotel
Cabaret
54 Below (▷ panel, 134)
Classical Music
Carnegie Hall
Jazz
Birdland

Live Music
Best Buy Theater
Madison Square Garden
Theater/Performance
The New Victory Theater
New World Stages
Radio City Music Hall
Signature Theatre
TV Show Recording
The Tonight Show
    starring Jimmy Fallon

Upper East Side and Central Park

Bars
Auction House
Roof Garden Café and Martini Bar
    at the Met
Stone Rose Lounge
Comedy
Dangerfield's
Jazz
Café Carlyle
Literary Events/Readings
92nd Street Y
Theater/Performance
Florence Gould Hall
Shakespeare in the Park

Upper West Side

Cinema
Lincoln Plaza Cinema
Classical Music
David Geffen Hall
Cathedral of St. John the Divine
The Metropolitan Opera
Comedy
Stand Up NY
Dance
David H. Koch Theater
Jazz
Dizzy's Club Coca Cola
Smoke
Live Music
Beacon Theatre
Theater/Performance
Symphony Space

Entertainment A-Z

92ND STREET Y
www.92Y.org
A varied program of events is held here including readings by renowned authors, folk music, jazz and lectures on a range of subjects.
🔲 E4 ✉ 1395 Lexington Avenue/92nd Street ☎ 212/415-5500 🚇 6 96th Street

ARLENE'S GROCERY
www.arlenesgrocery.net
This is one of the best rock clubs in the city, where hot new bands make their name.
🔲 G18 ✉ 95 Stanton Street, between Ludlow and Orchard streets ☎ 212/358-1633 🚇 F, M 2nd Avenue

AUCTION HOUSE
With sumptouous red velvet drapes, a fireplace, sofas and candlelight, this is more suited to a romantic drink than a rowdy night out. The no-furs, no-sneakers dress code gives an idea of the casual-chic ambience.
🔲 F4 ✉ 300 E 89th Street/Second Avenue ☎ 212/427-4458 🚇 4, 5, 6 86th Street

BARRAMUNDI
www.barramundiny.com
Woodsy decor, Aussie beers and a new flavor of infused vodka every week attract a neighborhood crowd to this Lower East Side hangout.
🔲 G18 ✉ 67 Clinton Street near Rivington Street ☎ 212/529-6999 🚇 F, J, Z Delancey Street–Essex Street

Check out the cocktails

BEACH AT GOVERNORS ISLAND
www.governorsbeachclub.com
This summer venue for live events with bars, a café and beer garden has views of the Manhattan skyline as you boogie to DJs and big-name bands.
🔲 Off map ✉ Governors Island ☎ 212/896-4600 ⛴ Ferry from Battery Maritime Building Slip at 10 South Street 🚇 1 South Ferry, R Whiteall

BEACON THEATRE
www.beacontheatre.com
The Beacon is one of the premier venues in the city, featuring multi-night stands by established artists such as Bob Dylan and Tom Petty, as well as many rising stars.
🔲 B7 ✉ 2124 Broadway/74th Street ☎ 212/465-6500 🚇 1, 2, 3 72nd Street

---

COCKTAIL CULTURE

Cocktail culture is alive and well in the Big Apple. The Martini craze is here to stay—many lounges and bars offer long menus of creative concoctions. Elegant glassware is crucial. Atmospheres range from urban chic to clubby lounge to pubs. Neighborhood pubs, with more emphasis on beer and bourbon, are favorite watering holes. Or, instead of alcohol, visit one of New York's coffee bars.

Carnegie Hall

BEST BUY THEATER
www.bestbuytheater.com
This theater is a medium-size venue for medium-big acts in a great location in the center of Times Square.
➕ C11/D11 ✉ 1515 Broadway/44th Street ☎ 212/930-1950 🚇 1, 2, 3, 7, N, Q, R, S Times Square–42nd Street

BIRDLAND
www.birdlandjazz.com
Big names, big bands, John Coltrane tributes and Cubans are the rage here. The club was established in New York in 1949.
➕ C11 ✉ 315 W 44th Street/8th–9th avenues ☎ 212/581-3080 🚇 A, C, E 42nd Street–Port Authority Bus Terminal

BLUE NOTE
www.bluenote.net
Jazz artists from around the world play two shows nightly at this popular Village jazz club and restaurant.
➕ D17 ✉ 131 W 3rd Street/6th Avenue–MacDougal Street ☎ 212/475-8592 🚇 A, C, E, B, D, F 4th Street–Washington Square

CAFÉ CARLYLE
www.thecarlyle.com
This lounge in the elegant Carlyle Hotel was home to the great Bobby Short until his death in 2005, but his spirit lives on in the piano players, lounge singers and jazz bands. Be sure to look in at Bemelmans Bar, with its whimsical murals of Central Park by the artist Ludwig Bemelmans.
➕ E6 ✉ 35 E 76th Street, Madison Avenue ☎ 212/744-1600 🚇 6 77th Street

CAFÉ WHA?
www.cafewha.com
In business since the 1950s, this has been a hot spot ever since Bob Dylan and Jimi Hendrix used to hang out here. The Boss started his career here. It's still going strong with bands performing nightly and styles ranging from R&B, funk and jazz to soul and modern rock.
➕ D17 ✉ 115 MacDougal/Minetta Lane ☎ 212/254-3706 🚇 A, B, C, D, E, F, M 4th Street–Washington Square

CARNEGIE HALL
www.carnegiehall.org
This world-class recital hall features an eclectic program from classical artists to folk singers, world music and pop. With so much choice, you are bound to find a concert that appeals to you.
➕ D9 ✉ 881 7th Avenue/57th Street ☎ 212/247-7800 🚇 N, R 57th Street; E 7th Avenue

CATHEDRAL OF ST. JOHN THE DIVINE
www.stjohndivine.org
The cathedral provides a varied program of liturgical, cultural and civic events.

🔲 B1　✉ 1047 Amsterdam Avenue/112th Street　☎ 212/316-7540　🚇 1 Cathedral Parkway–110th Street

CHERRY LANE THEATRE
www.cherrylanetheatre.org

This historic theater in Greenwich Village presents a vibrant program of landmark plays and works by emerging playwrights.

🔲 C17　✉ 38 Commerce Street between Barrow and Bedford streets　☎ 212/989-2020　🚇 1 Christopher Street–Sheridan Square

CITY WINERY
www.citywinery.com/newyork

Everything from intimate evenings with singer-songwriters to gourmet cooking demonstrations take place here. It's a fully functioning winery, too, with tastings and a shop.

🔲 D18　✉ 55 Varick Street/Vandam Street　☎ 212/608-0555　🚇 C, E Spring Street; 1 Houston

COMEDY CELLAR
www.comedycellar.com

A cozy Greenwich Village spot, this attracts well-known comedians from time to time. The intimate nature of the venue means you are quite likely to find you are part of the show, so be warned.

🔲 D17　✉ 117 MacDougal Street, between W 3rd Street and Minetta Lane and 130 W 3rd Street　☎ 212/254-3480　🚇 A, B, C, D, E, F, M 4th Street–Washington Square

DANGERFIELD'S
www.dangerfields.com

This comedy club, established in 1969, is still going strong with claims to be the oldest in the world. Those who have performed here include Jay Leno and Jim Carrey.

🔲 F9　✉ 1118 1st Avenue/61st Street　☎ 212/593-1650　🚇 4, 5, 6 59th Street

DAVID GEFFEN HALL
www.lincolncenter.org

In 2015, mogul David Geffen donated $100 million to rename and revamp concert venue Avery Fisher Hall, home to the New York Philharmonic. It is also home to concerts and recitals.

🔲 B8　✉ 10 Lincoln Center Plaza, Columbus Avenue/65th Street　☎ 212/875-5030　🚇 1 66th Street–Lincoln Center

DAVID H. KOCH THEATER
www.davidhkochtheater.com
www.nycballet.com

This sumptuous auditorium is the home of the New York City Ballet, which performs September through to June.

🔲 B8　✉ 20 Lincoln Center Plaza at 63rd Street　☎ 212/496-0600　🚇 1 66th Street–Lincoln Center

THE DEAD RABBIT GROCERY AND GROG
www.deadrabbitnyc.com

Every drink on the Dead Rabbit's extensive upstairs menu is historically sourced, giving patrons a flavor of old New York.

🔲 E23　✉ 30 Water Street/Broad Street　☎ 646/422-7906　🚇 1 South Ferry, R Whitehall

DIZZY'S CLUB COCA COLA
www.jazz.org/dizzys
Jazz at Lincoln Center's intimate club is—in the spirit of Dizzy Gillespie—designed to ensure that performers and spectators alike relaaaaax. There are After Hours sets Tuesday through Saturday.
✚ C9 ✉ Time Warner Center at Broadway/60th Street, 5th floor ☎ 212/258-9595 🚇 A, B, C, D, 1 59th Street–Columbus Circle

FILM FORUM
www.filmforum.com
New York's best revival house shows everything from silent films (complete with live accompaniment) to independent premieres, documentaries and classics.
✚ D18 ✉ 209 W Houston Street/Varick Street ☎ 212/727-8110 🚇 1 Houston Street

FLORENCE GOULD HALL
www.fiaf.org
Associated with the Alliance Française, this concert hall stages music, dance, jazz and readings with a French theme.
✚ E9 ✉ 55 E 59th Street/Park–Madison avenues ☎ 212/355-6160 🚇 N, R 5th Avenue–59th Street

FOUR SEASONS HOTEL
www.fourseasons.com/newyork
I. M. Pei design, a smooth vibe and a great Martini menu make this lobby bar an excellent choice for cocktails.
✚ E9 ✉ 57 E 57th Street/Madison Avenue ☎ 212/758-5700 🚇 4, 5, 6 Lexington Avenue–59th Street

GOTHAM COMEDY CLUB
www.gothamcomedyclub.com
Gotham showcases top stars as well as up-and-coming comedians.
✚ C14 ✉ 208 W 23rd Street/7th Avenue ☎ 212/367-9000 🚇 N, R, 1 23rd Street; F, Path 23rd Street

JOE'S PUB
www.joespub.com
The red velvet bar and performance space always has an interesting line-up of singers, comedians, magicians and burlesque artists.
✚ E16 ✉ The Public Theater, 425 Lafayette Street/Astor Place ☎ 212/967-7555 🚇 N, R 8th Street–NYU; 6 Astor Place

LINCOLN PLAZA CINEMA
www.lincolnplazacinema.com
Several screens show successful first runs and also foreign movies.
✚ B8 ✉ 1886 Broadway/63rd Street ☎ 212/757-2280 🚇 1 66th Street–Lincoln Center

MADISON SQUARE GARDEN
www.thegarden.com
The giant concrete circle is one of the city's major venues for music

---

CABARET
The term has undergone so many image overhauls, it's now settled into being a catch-all for entertainment options ranging from off-Broadway cabaret theater and downtown crooners sitting around the piano bar at Duplex (✉ 61 Christopher Street ☎ 212/255-5438, www.theduplex.com) to the Broadway supper club at 54 Below (☎ 254 W 54th Street, ☎ 646/476-3551, www.54below.com). Joe's Pub (above) is among the venues that offer what you might call classic, though modernized, cabaret.

and sporting events. For the box office enter the Main Ticket Lobby at 7th Avenue and 32nd Street.
🚩 C13   ✉ 4 Pennsylvania Plaza   ☎ 212/465-6741   🚇 1, 2, 3 34th Street–Penn Station

MCSORLEY'S OLD ALE HOUSE

New York's oldest saloon (1854) draws a crowd with its sawdust-covered floors, coal-burning stove and working-class history.
🚩 F16   ✉ 15 E 7th Street/3rd Avenue   ☎ 212/473-9148   🚇 6 Astor Place

MERCURY LOUNGE

www.mercuryloungenyc.com
Its laid-back atmosphere attracts eclectic performers.
🚩 F17   ✉ 217 E Houston Street/Essex Street   ☎ 212/260-4700   🚇 F 2nd Avenue

THE METROPOLITAN OPERA

www.metopera.org
The gala openings at this world-class opera house rank among the most glamorous of the city's cultural events. Visit the website early in the day for same day rush tickets. The box office is at the north end of the front lobby. The season runs from October to April.
🚩 B8   ✉ 30 Lincoln Center   ☎ 212/362-6000   🚇 1 66th Street–Lincoln Center

THE NEW VICTORY THEATER

www.newvictory.org
If you have kids (over five) in tow, there'll be something here to thrill them and keep them entertained.
🚩 C11   ✉ 209 W 42nd Street/7th–8th avenues   ☎ 646/223-3010   🚇 1, 2, 3, 7, N, R, Q Times Square–42nd Street

NEW WORLD STAGES

www.newworldstages.com
Check out the top off-Broadway productions, from musicals to kids' shows, at this state-of-the-art theatrical venue.
🚩 C10   ✉ 340 W 50th Street/8th Avenue   ☎ 646-871-1730   🚇 C, E 50th Street

PARKSIDE LOUNGE

www.parksidelounge.net
Parkside hosts live music, stand-up and karaoke, as well as people just having a beer. It's open until 4am, and is a relaxed and unpretentious place.
🚩 G17   ✉ 317 E Houston Street/Attorney Avenue   ☎ 212/673-6270   🚇 F, M 2nd Avenue

ENTERTAINMENT

OUT IN CENTRAL PARK

Central Park is a welcoming park. For those who crave physical activity there's lots to do.

Bike Riding You can rent a no-frills bicycle.

Rowing Rent rowboats from the Loeb Boathouse and venture out on the Lake.

Ice Skating Wollman Rink rents skates in winter and becomes an amusement park in summer.

Running The park is the most popular place for running and jogging.

PETE'S TAVERN

www.petestavern.com

A favorite with locals, this fine 1864 Gramercy Park Victorian saloon has a welcoming feel.

✚ E15 ✉ 129 E 18th Street/Irving Place ☎ 212/473-7676 🚇 L, N, R, 4, 6 14th Street–Union Square

THE PORTERHOUSE AT FRAUNCES TAVERN

www.frauncestavern.com

This 18th-century watering hole, where George Washington bade goodbye to his officers after the Revolutionary War, is now the first stateside branch of Dublin's Porterhouse Brewing Company. It has fine ales, stouts, guest beers and an adjoining restaurant.

✚ E22 ✉ 54 Pearl Street/Broad Street ☎ 212/968-1776 🚇 N, R Whitehall Street

Famous since the 1930s

RADIO CITY MUSIC HALL

www.radiocity.com

This landmark art deco theater, which opened in 1932, hosts several music shows a year. You can also take an hour-long tour.

✚ D10 ✉ 1260 6th Avenue/50th Street ☎ 212/247-4777 🕐 Varied. Tours daily 11–3 🚇 B, D, F, M 40th–50th streets–Rockefeller Center

ROOF GARDEN CAFÉ AND MARTINI BAR AT THE MET

www.metmuseum.org

You can get cocktails and simple food on this rooftop terrace dotted with sculpture. Access is by elevators on the far southwest corner. It's open May through late fall (weather permitting).

✚ D5 ✉ Metropolitan Museum of Art, 1000 5th Avenue/82nd Street ☎ 212/535-7710 🚇 6 86th Street

SHAKESPEARE IN THE PARK

www.publictheater.org

The Shakespeare festival is a highlight of summer in Central Park. Line up for free tickets as soon as possible, or chance your luck with virtual ticketing.

✚ C6 ✉ Delacorte Theater in Central Park, 81st Street (west side) ☎ 212/539-8500 🚇 B, C 81st Street

SIGNATURE THEATRE

www.signaturetheatre.org

Every season at this off-Broadway house, designed by Frank Gehry, has a new playwright-in-residence from the first ranks of American theater. Even those not here for a show will enjoy the café/bar in the upstairs lobby.

🚼 B11 ✉ 480 W 42nd Street/10th Avenue ☎ 2212/244-7529 🚇 A, C, E 42nd Street

SING SING KARAOKE
www.karaokesingsing.com
You'll be able to sing your heart out in this popular karaoke venue.

🚼 G17 ✉ 81 Avenue A/E 5th and 6th Street ☎ 212/674-0700 🚇 F, M Lower East Side-2nd Avenue

SMOKE
www.smokejazz.com
Plush couches adorn this intimate jazz lounge, which hosts local and well-known names.

🚼 B2 ✉ 2751 Broadway/106th Street ☎ 212/864-6662 🚇 1 103rd Street

S.O.B.'S
www.sobs.com
The Latin beat keeps you dancing at the tropically themed nightclub Sounds of Brazil. Hear African, reggae and other island music.

🚼 D18 ✉ 204 Varick Street/Houston Street ☎ 212/243-4940 🚇 1 Houston Street

STAND UP NY
www.standupny.com
Aspiring comics try out their new routines in this traditional comedy club.

🚼 B6 ✉ 236 W 78th Street/Broadway ☎ 212/595-0850 🚇 1 79th Street

STONE ROSE LOUNGE
www.stoneroselounge.com
Enjoy impressively designed surroundings, fine food and drink, and stunning views of Central Park and Broadway.

🚼 C9 ✉ Time Warner Center, Columbus Circle ☎ 212/823-9769 🚇 A, B, C, D 59th Street–Columbus Circle

SYMPHONY SPACE
www.symphonyspace.org
Head here for storytelling, readings, children's theater, music, dance, film and more.

🚼 B4 ✉ 2537 Broadway/95th Street ☎ 212/864-5400 🚇 1, 2, 3 96th Street

THE TONIGHT SHOW STARRING JIMMY FALLON
www.nbc.com/the-tonight-show
Upon taking the helm of *The Tonight Show*, Jimmy Fallon moved it back to New York City for the first time in decades. Take your chance at same-day standby tickets by lining up before 9am under the NBC Studios marquee on 49th Street.

🚼 D10 ✉ 30 Rockfeller Plaza/49th Street ☎ 212/664-3056 🚇 B, D, F, M 47–50 Streets–Rockefeller Center

WHITE HORSE TAVERN
www.whitehorsetavern.com
This sprawling 1880s bar was the last watering hole of Welsh poet Dylan Thomas.

🚼 C16 ✉ 567 Hudson Street/11th Street ☎ 212/989-3956 🚇 1 Christopher Street–Sheridan Square

---

BIG IN NEW YORK

From the elegance of a grand opera to the excitement of avant-garde performance art, New York spectacles are world-class (even the flops). Broadway shows can be expensive, but nothing transports audiences like a great multimillion-dollar musical or an intense performance by a drama diva. Be sure to reserve tickets in advance for the most popular shows.

Eat

There are places to eat across the city to suit all tastes and budgets. In this section establishments are listed alphabetically.

EAT

Introduction

From basic diners serving trademark large portions to über-trendy chefs and chic restaurants showcasing world cuisine, New York really can claim to offer something to suit every taste, diet and budget.

Around the World

In this global melting pot it's almost impossible not to find just about every cuisine in the world. The city hosts an abundance of celebrity chefs, but also hole-in-the-wall eateries featuring almost every imaginable cuisine. To get a flavor of the city's culinary heritage check out a food tour such as the one offered by Foods of NY tours (www.foodsofny.com).

A Day's Dining

No one does breakfast or brunch like Manhattanites (especially on weekends) so make for Greenwich Village or SoHo, grab a copy of the *New York Times* and just chill over your choice of eggs, pancakes or waffles and limitless coffee. For lunch, try a Jewish deli for plenty of atmosphere and gargantuan sandwiches; make for the Dining Concourse on the lower level of Grand Central Terminal (▷ 145); or, if you're downtown, Chinatown or Little Italy should help keep you fueled for the rest of the day's shopping or sightseeing. Dinner in New York can be as casual or as stylish as your mood and budget dictate.

TAXES, TIPPING AND FINANCIAL MATTERS

A sales tax of 8.875 percent will be added to your dining bill. The minimum tip (with good service) is 15 percent; people often double the tax for a 17.75 percent tip. Many restaurants offer fixed-price menus, which are good value. Watch for New York Restaurant Week, held twice a year in winter and summer. This special promotion offers a three-course menu at reduced rates for lunch and dinner at many restaurants; this deal is often extended so it's always worth checking if it's available.

From top: Pancakes with maple syrup in a New York diner; the city has some great pizzerias; Café Boulud, a top restaurant; cheeseburger with fries

EAT

Directory

Lower Manhattan

Asian
Dim Sum Go Go
Mission Chinese
Nobu

Casual
The Bailey Pub & Brasserie
Bubby's
Delicatessen
Schillers

Classic NY
Katz's Deli
Odeon (▷ panel, 142)

Downtown and Chelsea

Asian
Fatty Crab

Contemporary
Gotham Bar and Grill
North Square
The Spotted Pig

French/American
Almond

Italian
Del Posto

Mexican
Mary Ann's

Polish/Ukrainian
Veselka

Midtown

Asian
Kajitsu (▷ panel, 144)

Casual
Grand Central Terminal Dining
    Concourse (▷ panel, 145)
John's Pizzeria

Classic NY
'21' Club
Four Seasons
Oyster Bar

Contemporary
Le Bernardin
Casa Lever
Per Se

European
Uncle Nick's

Upper East Side and Central Park

Casual
Jackson Hole
Serendipity 3

Classic NY
Loeb Boathouse

Contemporary
Café Boulud
Daniel

European
Café Sabarsky

Middle Eastern
Persepolis

Upper West Side

Casual
Barney Greengrass
Boat Basin Café

Contemporary
Jean-Georges
Ouest
Picholine
Tolani Wine Restaurant

Italian
Carmine's

Farther Afield

Casual
Grimaldi's

Classic NY
Peter Luger

Contemporary
Blue Ribbon
Grocery
Henry's End
River Café

EAT

Eating A-Z

EAT

PRICES

Prices are approximate, based on a 3-course meal for one person.

$$$	over $60
$$	$40–$60
$	under $40

'21' CLUB $$$

www.21club.com

With a history spanning more than eight decades, this eatery doffs a cap to its speakeasy days. Choose from fixed-price menus or an extensive à la carte featuring lobster, steak, salmon and much more. The '21' burger is a favorite.

🔲 D10 ✉ 21 W 52nd Street/5th–6th avenues ☎ 212/582–7200 🕐 Tue–Fri lunch, Mon–Sat dinner 🚇 B, D, F, M 47th–50th streets–Rockefeller Center

ALMOND $$

www.almondnyc.com

This warm and friendly American bistro uses the freshest ingredients from farm to table. The sea scallops are not to be missed, and it seems a shame to have to share the apple cinnamon crisp for two. Reservations here are essential.

🔲 E14 ✉ 12 E 22nd Street/Broadway–Park Avenue ☎ 212/228-7557 🕐 Daily lunch and dinner, weekend brunch 🚇 R 23rd Street

THE BAILEY PUB & BRASSERIE $–$$

www.thebaileynyc.com

Just off Wall Street, this is a big hit with the Financial District crowd. The bar, which stays open until 1am, serves British pub-style food. The Brasserie offers excellent yet inexpensive meals, from salads and sandwiches through to steaks and a *plat du jour*.

🔲 E22 ✉ 52 William Street ☎ 212/859-2200 🕐 Daily breakfast, lunch and dinner, weekend brunch 🚇 A, C Broadway–Nassau; 2, 3, 4, 5 Wall Street

BARNEY GREENGRASS $

www.barneygreengrass.com

An Upper West Side tradition since 1929, this is frantic on weekends, when locals feast on huge platters of smoked fish—whitefish, sable, sturgeon and lox—or sandwiches made with similar ingredients.

🔲 B5 ✉ 541 Amsterdam Avenue/86th Street ☎ 212/724-4707 🕐 Tue–Fri 8.30–4, Sat–Sun 8.30–5 🚇 1 86th Street

LE BERNARDIN $$$

www.le-bernardin.com

Frenchman Eric Ripert is acknowledged to be the fish maestro. Exquisite, inventive dishes are served by super-attentive waiters.

🔲 D10 ✉ 155 W 51st Street/7th Avenue ☎ 212/554-1515 🕐 Mon–Fri lunch, Mon–Sat dinner 🚇 B, D, F, M 47th–50th streets–Rockefeller Center

ODEON $$

After celebrating its quarter-century in 2005 with all the '80s faces that made it the first hot spot of the *Bright Lights, Big City* age, this art deco-style restaurant still outdoes half the new *boîtes* in town. Its tiled floors, dim lighting, happy bar area and open-most-hours welcome are some reasons why—that and the always-reliable nouvelle-American cooking.

🔲 D20 ✉ 145 West Broadway/Thomas Street ☎ 212/233-0507, www.theodeonrestaurant.com 🕐 Daily lunch and dinner, Sat–Sun brunch and dinner 🚇 A, C Chambers Street

BLUE RIBBON $$

www.blueribbonrestaurants.com

There's a Manhattan feel to this huge modern-American favorite in Brooklyn, and that's not surprising, since it has an older sister there (97 Sullivan Street/Prince Street), liked by off-duty chefs. It combines creative and comfort food.

➕ See map ▷ 111 ✉ 280 5th Avenue/1st Street, Brooklyn ☎ 718/840-0404 ⏰ Daily dinner 🚇 R Union Street

BOAT BASIN CAFÉ $

www.boatbasincafe.com

It's hard to find this café serving diner-style food on the banks of the Hudson, but if you do, sit at a terrace table. The view is dazzling.

➕ A6 ✉ W 79th Street/Hudson River ☎ 212/496-5542 ⏰ Late Mar–Oct (weather permitting) daily lunch and dinner 🚇 1 79th Street

BUBBY'S $

www.bubbys.com

A Tribeca favorite, Bubby's serves all-American BLTs, chicken clubs, meat loaf and fries, followed by pies (for example chocolate or

peanut butter). Expect a wait for the popular weekend brunch.

➕ D19 ✉ 120 Hudson Street ☎ 212/219-0666 ⏰ Open 24 hours, except Tue 12am–7am 🚇 1, 9 Franklin Street; A, C, E Canal Street

CAFÉ BOULUD $$–$$$

www.cafeboulud.com

This Daniel Boulud restaurant has classical, seasonal and ethnic influences. You will find *pot au feu*, *bouillabaisse* and entrées inspired by Spain, Morocco and Vietnam.

➕ E6 ✉ 20 E 76th Street/5th–Madison avenues ☎ 212/772-2600 ⏰ Daily breakfast, lunch, dinner; Sun brunch, closed public holidays 🚇 6 77th Street

CAFÉ SABARSKY $–$$

neuegallerie.org

The restaurant in the Neue Galerie has New York's premier Austrian chef, Kurt Gutenbrunner, at the helm. You can also just drop in for coffee and cake.

➕ E5 ✉ Neue Galerie New York, 1048 5th Avenue/86th Street ☎ 212/288-0665 ⏰ Mon and Wed 9–6, Thu–Sun 9–9, closed Tue 🚇 4, 5, 6 86th Street

Bubby's in Tribeca is a favorite choice for weekend brunch

EAT

CARMINE'S $$

www.carminesnyc.com

This beloved, raucous place serves Sicilian-Italian dishes family-style—huge platters to share. It's not for picky foodies, but it's fun.

🞤 B4 ✉ 2450 Broadway/90th Street ☎ 212/362-2200 🕔 Daily lunch and dinner 🚇 1, 2, 3 96th Street–Broadway

CASA LEVER $$–$$$

www.casalever.com

The ocean liner-esque design is the star at this restaurant, downstairs in the 1952 Lever House building on Park Avenue, but it would be worth visiting for chef Mario Danieli's contemporary menu alone. It serves twists on northern Italian classics.

🞤 E10 ✉ 390 Park Avenue/53rd Street ☎ 212/888-2700 🕔 Mon–Fri breakfast, lunch and dinner, Sat brunch and dinner, closed Sun 🚇 E, M Lexington Avenue–53rd Street; 6 51st Street

DANIEL $$$

www.danielnyc.com

This formal restaurant serves exquisitely restrained, modern French dishes—opt for the six-course tasting menu to appreciate fully chef Daniel Boulud's brilliance. Dessert arrives with its own basket of warm madeleines.

🞤 E8 ✉ 60 E 65th Street/Madison–Park avenues ☎ 212/288-0033 🕔 Mon–Sat dinner, closed Sun 🚇 6 68th Street–Hunter College

DEL POSTO $$$

www.delposto.com

Mario Batali, New York's rotundly ebullient TV-friendly patron saint of interesting Italian food, may be known for creating rustic dishes in a casual ambience, but this is a swanky, deco-looking, big-night-out restaurant, with piano player, tableside preparations and valet parking. It works beautifully.

🞤 B15 ✉ 85 10th Avenue/16th Street ☎ 212/497-8090 🕔 Mon–Fri lunch and dinner, Sat–Sun dinner 🚇 A, C, E, L 14th Street

DELICATESSEN $

www.delicatessennyc.com

In need of some comfort food? At this funky SoHo restaurant you can start with Grandma's meatloaf then finish off with milk and cookies.

🞤 D18 ✉ 54 Prince Street/Lafayette Street ☎ 212/226-0211 🕔 Daily lunch and dinner 🚇 N, R Prince Street

DIM SUM GO GO $

www.dimsumgogo.com

This small, vegetarian-friendly restaurant is a great choice in Chinatown. Delicious dim sum feature such fillings as jicama, lotus root, bamboo heart, snow pea leaf and seafood. There's a full menu of meat and seafood dishes too.

🞤 F20 ✉ 5 East Broadway, between Catherine Street and Chatham Square ☎ 212/732-0797 🕔 Daily lunch and dinner 🚇 F East Broadway

ZEN VEGGIES

The only vegetarian restaurant in New York to be awarded a Michelin star, Kajitsu ($$$) emphasizes Japanese shojin cuisine through its multi-course tasting menus. The choices change each month, with emphasis on seasonal delights. Reserve well in advance.

🞤 E12 ✉ 129 E 39th Street/Lexington Avenue ☎ 212/228-4873 🕔 Tue–Sat lunch and dinner, Sun dinner 🚇 4, 5, 6, 7, S 42nd Street-Grand Central.

FATTY CRAB $$

www.fattycrab.com

Malaysia meets Manhattan in this unpretentious place. It's not exclusively seafood—the short ribs rendang is extremely good. Great wines and cocktails complement the cuisine.

✚ C16 ✉ 643 Hudson Street, between Horatio and Gansevoort ☎ 212/352-3592 ⊙ Daily lunch and dinner 🚇 1

FOUR SEASONS $$$

www.fourseasonsrestaurant.com

The Four Seasons changed the face of New York dining when it opened in1959. Sample dishes include Maryland crabmeat cakes in mustard sauce, and filet of bison with foie gras and Perigord black truffle.

✚ E10 ✉ 99 E 52nd Street/Park–Lexington avenues ☎ 212/754-9494 ⊙ Mon–Fri lunch and dinner, Sat dinner only, closed Sun 🚇 6 51st Street

GOTHAM BAR AND GRILL $$$

www.gothambarandgrill.com

This restaurant epitomizes New York grandeur, with world-class dishes such as wild striped bass with *haricots verts*. The soaring space is beautifully light and airy.

✚ E16 ✉ 12 E 12th Street/5th Avenue ☎ 212/620-4020 ⊙ Mon–Fri lunch and dinner, Sat–Sun dinner only 🚇 L, N, R, Q, 4, 5, 6 14th Street–Union Square

GRIMALDI'S $

www.grimaldis.com

With one of the few coal brick-ovens left in the city, Grimaldi's pizza restaurant dates back to 1905 and has attracted many celebrities, including Frank Sinatra. Constant lines are testament to its reputation. No credit cards.

GRAND CENTRAL

Here are some highlights at the Dining Concourse at Grand Central Terminal:
Two Boots for standard and creative pizza.
Café Spice for curries.
Junior's is a great diner with peerless cheesecake.
Magnolia Bakery for scrumptious pastries.
Manhattan Chili Company makes a mean bowl o' red from all-natural ingredients.
Mendy's Kosher Delicatessen does knishes and pastrami-on-rye.

✚ H21 ✉ 1 Front Street (under Brooklyn Bridge) ☎ 718/858-4300 ⊙ Daily lunch and dinner 🚇 A, C High Street; 2 3 Clark Street

GROCERY $$$

www.thegroceryrestaurant.com

A tiny chef-owned restaurant with changing nouvelle-American menus. The inside is homey and the tree-shaded garden is lovely.

✚ See map ▷ 111 ✉ 288 Smith Street/between Sackett and Union, Brooklyn ☎ 718/596-3335 ⊙ Tue–Sat dinner, closed Sun–Mon 🚇 F, G Carroll Street

Sensational sushi

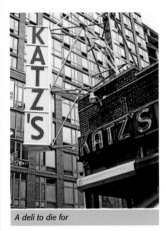
A deli to die for

HENRY'S END $$

www.henrysend.com

This neighborhood favorite in Brooklyn has high ceilings, brick walls and an open kitchen. The menu features seasonal fish and locally sourced meat and produce, but the highlight is the Wild Game Festival (winter to spring), plus an award-winning wine list.

➕ H22 ✉ 44 Henry Street/Cranberry Street, Brooklyn Heights ☎ 718/834-1776 🕐 Daily dinner 🚇 A, C High Street; 2, 3 Clark Street

JACKSON HOLE $

www.jacksonholeburgers.com

This small chain of burger places is useful when all you want is a hefty sandwich in a child-friendly, no-frills environment.

➕ E4 ✉ 1270 Madison Avenue/91st Street ☎ 212/427-2820 🚇 4, 5, 6 86th Street ➕ F8 ✉ 232 E 64th Street/2nd Avenue ☎ 212/371-7187 🕐 Daily breakfast, lunch and dinner 🚇 6 68th Street–Hunter College

JEAN-GEORGES $$$

www.jean-georges.com

One of the world's great chefs, Alsace native Jean Georges Vongerichten is known for his refined, full-flavored Asian-accented cooking. The glass-walled minimalist rooms feel serene and special. Lunch here is a (relative) bargain. Don't miss the molten-center chocolate cake.

➕ C9 ✉ 1 Central Park West/60th Street ☎ 212/299-3900 🕐 Mon–Sat lunch and dinner, closed Sun 🚇 A, C, B, D 1 59th Street–Columbus Circle

JOHN'S PIZZERIA $

www.johnspizzerianyc.com

This converted church has one of just a handful of coal brick-ovens left in the city. It's a great spot to head to for a pre- or post-theater pizza.

➕ C11 ✉ 260 W 44th Street ☎ 212/391-7560 🕐 Daily lunch and dinner 🚇 1, 2, 3, 7, N, Q, R Times Square–42nd Street

NEW YORK RESTAURANT WEEK

The best dining deal in town is no longer a mere seven-day affair. New York Restaurant Week now takes place twice a year, and lasts for up to a month each winter and summer (dates vary, check website below for details). Participating restaurants offer three-course lunches and dinners at a set price. The cost of your drinks, tax and tip are extra. This event offers a great chance to dine at some of New York's best and hottest restaurants for a fraction of the normal price. The menus are designed to show off their classic dishes and cooking styles. Check out the dates and restaurants at www.nycgo.com, and book ahead—the best tables go fast!

KATZ'S DELI $

www.katzsdelicatessen.com
The site of the hilarious climactic
scene in *When Harry Met Sally* is
the last deli in a once thriving
Jewish neighborhood. Opened
in 1888, it upholds traditions such
as plain surroundings, and knishes
and pastrami sandwiches.
➕ G17 ✉ 205 E Houston Street/Ludlow
Street ☎ 212/254-2246 ◉ Daily breakfast, lunch and dinner 🚇 F, M Lower East
Side–2nd Avenue

LOEB BOATHOUSE $$

www.thecentralparkboathouse.com
Leave hectic Manhattan behind at
this lakeside place in Central Park.
The food is contemporary
American but the view is the main
reason for coming. The cocktail
deck gets busy in summer.
Reservations are advised.
➕ D7 ✉ Central Park, nearest to E 72nd
Street entrance ☎ 212/517-2233
◉ Mon–Fri lunch and dinner, Sat–Sun
brunch and dinner, lunch only Dec–Mar
🚇 6 68th Street–Hunter College

MARY ANN'S $

www.maryannsmexican.com
Come here for homemade
Mexican food, including fresh
tortillas and dishes you won't find
at your average Tex-Mex, a great
atmosphere and margaritas by the
pint. You can only pay with cash.
➕ C15 ✉ 116 8th Avenue/16th Street
☎ 212/633-0877 ◉ Daily lunch and
dinner 🚇 C, E 14th Street; L 8th Avenue

MISSION CHINESE $$$

www.mcfny.com
Award-winning chef Danny
Bowien's Mission Chinese opened
its first NYC branch in 2012. Its
current home came with a built-in

pizza oven, so Bowien added the
Italian staple to his menu of mostly
northern Chinese cuisine. No
reservations here, so come early.
➕ G19 ✉ 171 East Broadway/Essex Street
☎ 212/529-8800 ◉ Tue–Sun dinner only
🚇 F East Broadway, J, M, Z Essex Street

NOBU $$$

www.noburestaurants.com
It is difficult to get a reservation at
this Japanese shrine, part owned
by Robert de Niro, but you'll be
rewarded by the memorable food
and gorgeous setting. Choose the
sea urchin tempura or fresh
yellowtail sashimi with jalapeno.
➕ D19 ✉ 105 Hudson Street/Franklin
Street ☎ 212/219-0500 ◉ Mon–Fri lunch
and dinner, Sat–Sun dinner only
🚇 1 Franklin Street

NORTH SQUARE $$

www.northsquareny.com
Chef Yoel Cruz's inventive cooking
focuses on Mediterranean dishes.
The atmosphere is relaxed, and
dishes such as coriander-crusted
yellowfin tuna are sublime. The
Sunday jazz brunch has featured
Norah Jones, who used to wait
tables here.
➕ D16 ✉ 103 Waverly Place/MacDougal
Street ☎ 212/254-1200 ◉ Mon–Fri
breakfast, lunch and dinner, Sat–Sun brunch
and dinner 🚇 A, C, E, B, D, F, M West 4th
Street–Washington Square

> ### BRUNCH
> It's hard to imagine what New Yorkers did
> before the invention of brunch. These
> days the weekend noontime meal can be
> everything from a basic omelet to a multi-
> course culinary adventure, and it needn't
> be consumed before noon. A 2pm brunch
> with mimosas (Buck's Fizz) is just fine.

OUEST $$–$$$

www.ouestny.com

This place revitalized the Upper West Side dining scene with its red booths and Euro-American comfort dishes of chef Tom Valenti. His lamb shanks are legendary.

🚇 B5 ✉ 2315 Broadway/83rd Street ☎ 212/580-8700 🕐 Daily dinner 🚊 1 86th Street

OYSTER BAR $$

www.oysterbarny.com

Some reports suggest this 1913 vaulted room in Grand Central Terminal may be resting on past glories, but for a thoroughly New York experience it's hard to beat.

🚇 E11 ✉ Grand Central Terminal, lower level ☎ 212/490-6650 🕐 Mon–Sat lunch and dinner, closed Sun 🚊 4, 5, 6, 7 Grand Central–42nd Street

PER SE $$$

www.perseny.com

If you want to know what all the fuss is about, reserve *way, way* ahead for Thomas Keller's idiosyncratic cuisine, such as terrine of foie gras and veal cheek or smoked river sturgeon with violet artichokes, peas and mint cream. Great views from the window tables.

🚇 C9 ✉ Time Warner Center, 10 Columbus Circle, 4th floor/60th Street ☎ 212/823-9335 🕐 Daily dinner, Fri–Sun lunch 🚊 A, C, B, D, 1 59th Street–Columbus Circle

PERSEPOLIS $$

www.persepolisnewyork.com

Thai chef San Sethachutkul took to Persian cooking with great flair when he came to New York, and now serves some of the city's finest Middle Eastern cuisine. Try the delicious saffron-marinated rack of lamb.

🚇 F7 ✉ 1407 Second Avenue/73rd Street ☎ 212/535-1100 🕐 Daily lunch and dinner 🚊 6 Lexington Avenue

PETER LUGER $$$

www.peterluger.com

Peter Luger has been serving the city's best beef here to hungry New Yorkers since 1887. No need for embellishment, simply order hash browns and creamed spinach to accompany your steak. Reserve early. No credit cards.

🚇 See map ▷ 111 ✉ 178 Broadway/ Driggs Avenue, Brooklyn ☎ 718/387-7400 🕐 Daily lunch and dinner 🚊 J, Z Marcy Avenue

PICHOLINE $$$

www.picholinenyc.com

An elegant address for the inventive Mediterranean cuisine of Terrance Brennan. The standard of food served here remains as good as ever.

🚇 C8 ✉ 35 W 64th Street, between Central Park West and Broadway ☎ 212/724-8585 🕐 Daily dinner 🚊 1 66th Street–Lincoln Center

---

FOOD ON WHEELS

The lowly hot dog stand and pretzel cart have stepped up a notch. More than 3,000 gourmet food trucks now ply the streets of Manhattan, serving up a variety of tasty, healthy and inexpensive fare to busy New Yorkers on the go. Doling out everything from biryanis to Korean BBQ, organic salads to schnitzel and Belgian waffles, some have reached near-cult status. Trucks broadcast their locations to fans on Twitter, and there are websites and apps to help you find your favorite truck or see who's currently in your area.

RIVER CAFÉ $$$

www.rivercafe.com

For a special occasion (jackets required, guys) and drop-dead views across the East River to Manhattan, this is a treat. Classic international food ranges from caviar and wild rock lobster to rabbit and dumplings.

🔠 🔠 See map ▷ 111 ✉ 1 Water Street (under the Brooklyn Bridge) ☎ 718/522-5200 🕐 Mon–Sat lunch and dinner, Sun brunch and dinner 🚇 A, C High Street; 2, 3 Clark Street

SCHILLERS $–$$

www.schillersny.com

The man who brought France to Manhattan (Balthazar, Pastis) veers toward the Mitteleuropa deli here.

🔠 G18 ✉ 131 Rivington Street/Norfolk Street ☎ 212/260-4555 🕐 Daily breakfast/brunch, lunch, dinner 🚇 F 2nd Avenue

SERENDIPITY 3 $

www.serendipity3.com

This toy box cum candy store makes the original and best "Frozen Hot Chocolate," as well as burgers, soups and grills.

🔠 F9 ✉ 225 E 60th Street/2nd Avenue ☎ 212/838-3531 🕐 Daily lunch and dinner 🚇 4, 5, 6 59th Street

THE SPOTTED PIG $$

www.thespottedpig.com

You may have to wait for a table (you can't reserve) at this Michelin-starred, Anglo-style gastro pub. Order the *gnudi*, a ricotta-spinach gnocchi that chef April Bloomfield has made her own.

🔠 D16 ✉ 314 W 11th Street/Greenwich Avenue ☎ 212/620-0393 🕐 Daily lunch and dinner, Sat–Sun also brunch 🚇 1 Christopher Street

---

BAGEL PEOPLE

If NYC has a signature food, it might be the bagel. One top choice is Absolute Bagels (🔠 B2 ✉ 2788 Broadway/108th Street ☎ 212/932-2052), which serves classic flavors like sesame, pumpernickel, and poppy. To go truly old-school, visit Kossar's Bialys (🔠 G18 ✉ 367 Grand Street/Essex Street ☎ 212/473-4810), the only kosher purveyor of these oniony bagel-like breads still operating on the Lower East Side.

TOLANI WINE RESTAURANT $$

www.tolaninyc.com

Choose from a menu of classic combinations and global comfort food, with dishes like peri peri prawns or goat curry served on small plates for sharing.

🔠 B6 ✉ 410 Amsterdam Avenue/79th Street ☎ 212/873-6252 🕐 Mon–Fri dinner, Sat–Sun brunch and dinner 🚇 1 79th Street

UNCLE NICK'S $$

www.unclenicksgreekrestaurant.com

A fun atmosphere and hearty Greek cooking are hallmarks here. The seafood is straight off the dock.

🔠 B10 ✉ 747 9th Avenue/50th Street ☎ 212/245-7992 🕐 Daily lunch and dinner 🚇 C, E 50th Street

VESELKA $

www.veselka.com

Dine here at any time of day or night on Ukrainian and Polish soul food. The menu ranges from handmade *pierogi* (dumplings) to goulash and *blintzes*.

🔠 F16 ✉ 144 2nd Avenue/E 9th Street ☎ 212/228-9682 🕐 Daily 24 hours 🚇 6 Astor Place; F 2nd Avenue; R 8th Street

Sleep

With options ranging from the luxurious to simple budget hotels, New York has accommodations to suit everyone. In this section establishments are listed alphabetically.

SLEEP

Introduction

There are plenty of hotel rooms but it is hard to find a comfortable room under $150. If money is no object, reserve a room at the Four Seasons.

On a Budget
The fact of the matter is that lodging in New York on a budget can be tough and even budget chains can be pricey. Note that while outer-borough or airport hotels may be tempting, they can put you far away from sights and attractions. Many good hotels offer discounts: Monitor booking websites assiduously or consider a hotel alternative (▷ panel, below).

Luxury Living
You'll find first-class luxury hotels throughout the city, although many are in Midtown. Nearly every hotel room comes with air-conditioning, private bathroom, coffeemaker, cable TV, telephone and hair dryer, but top-class hotel rooms boast luxe fabrics and linens, high-tech electronics and high staff-to-guest ratios.

Prices
Today there is no such thing as a standard rack rate. Prices change with customer demand, so call the hotel and ask about the best available rate and special discounts. Alternatively, go online to discount services hotels.com, quikbook.com or hoteldiscounts.com. Note that taxes will be added to your bill, plus $3.50 occupancy tax on a standard room and 5.875 percent of the bill.

HOME AWAY FROM HOME
One way to stretch your travel budget is to consider a home stay or apartment swap. HomeExchange.com (for a fee) will help you swap homes with New Yorkers. VRBO.com is another reputable source for short-term apartment rentals.

From top: The Plunge Bar and Lounge at Hotel Gansevoort; guest room in The Shoreham; Crosby Street Hotel; clean lines at The Shoreham

SLEEP

Directory

Lower Manhattan

Budget
Cosmopolitan
Mid-Range
Off Soho Suites
Luxury
Crosby Street Hotel
Ritz-Carlton Battery Park

Downtown and Chelsea

Budget
Carlton Arms
Chelsea Lodge
Hotel 17
Mid-Range
Maritime Hotel
Washington Square
Luxury
Hotel Gansevoort
Inn at Irving Place

Midtown

Budget
Ameritania Hotel

Hotel Wolcott
Mid-Range
70 Park Avenue
The Algonquin (▷ panel, 155)
Casablanca
The Hudson
Jolly Madison Hotel
Library Hotel (▷ panel, 156)
Millennium Broadway
The Time
Luxury
Four Seasons
Mandarin Oriental
The Plaza
St. Regis
The Shoreham

Upper West Side

Budget
Hotel Belleclaire
Mid-Range
Excelsior
Hotel Beacon

SLEEP

Sleeping A–Z

PRICES

Prices are approximate and based on a double room for one night.

$$$	over $400
$$	$201–$400
$	$100–$200

70 PARK AVENUE $$

www.70parkave.com
The first foray into New York by boutique hotel pioneers Kimpton, this 205-room Murray Hill place has a quietly contemporary decor, luxurious extras such as touch-screen room service, a pillow menu, good sound systems and a special yoga channel on the huge flatscreen TV.

 E12 ✉ 70 Park Avenue/38th Street
☎ 212/973-2400 🍴 Silverleaf Tavern
🚇 4, 5, 6, 7, S Grand Central–42nd Street

AMERITANIA HOTEL $

www.ameritaniahotelnewyork.com
If you want to be in the heart of the theater district then the Ameritania provides mid-class accommodation with the added benefit of spacious common areas and lounge bar.

🔲 C10 ✉ 230 W 54th Street/Broadway
☎ 407/740-6442 🚇 D 55th Street; N, Q, R 57th Street–7th Avenue

CARLTON ARMS $

www.carltonarms.com

Decorated with crazy murals in the lobby and some of the rooms, this is one of New York's wackiest hotels. Amenities here are minimal but there is a communal atmosphere that makes travelers feel at home. As it says on the business card, "this ain't no Holiday Inn." The 54 comfortable rooms offer good-value accommodation.

🚹 F14 ✉ 160 E 25th Street/Lexington–3rd avenues ☎ 212/679-0680 🚇 6 23rd Street

CASABLANCA $$

www.casablancahotel.com

Moroccan prints and tiles make this small boutique hotel an oasis of color and style. Rooms range from cozy classics to premium kings and mini-suites, all with luxurious bath amenities and complimentary WiFi. Deluxe continental breakfast and passes to New York Sports Club are included.

🚹 D11 ✉ 147 W 43rd Street/7th Avenue ☎ 212/869-1212 🚇 N, Q, R, S, 1, 2, 3, 7, 9 Times Square–42nd Street

CHELSEA LODGE $

www.chelsealodge.com

The 22 guest rooms of this budget hotel in a brownstone building in the heart of Chelsea are clean and simple, and all come with a shower, sink, TV, and air-conditioning in summer and heating in winter. Bathrooms are shared, but for the location it's a bargain.

🚹 C15 ✉ 318 W 20th Street between 8th and 9th ☎ 212/243-4499 🚇 A, C, E 23rd Street; 1, 2 23rd Street

COSMOPOLITAN $

www.cosmohotel.com

No frills in any sense of the word exist at this 150-room, seven-story block in Tribeca. But, if you reckon the real estate rule applies to hotels, you'll love it—the location, location, location is prime. The clean, fully functional rooms vary a good deal in size, so if the hotel isn't full and you're not happy with the room you are shown, ask to see another one.

🚹 E20 ✉ 95 W Broadway/Chambers Street ☎ 212/566-1900 🚇 A, C Chambers Street

The bar in Crosby Street Hotel, a fashionable choice in SoHo

The Ty Warner Penthouse in the Four Seasons

SLEEP

CROSBY STREET HOTEL $$$

www.crosbystreethotel.com

This new kid on the block is from über-cool hoteliers Firmdale. In the heart of vibrant SoHo, the 86 rooms and suites over 11 floors have full-length warehouse-style windows. The interior design by Kit Kemp is fresh and contemporary, and the hotel has a gym, cinema and a sculpture garden, as well as a selection of one- and two-bed-room suites.

➕ E18 ✉ 79 Crosby Street, between Prince and Spring streets ☎ 212/226-6400 🚇 4, 6 Spring Street–Lafayette Street

EXCELSIOR $$

www.excelsiorhotelny.com

The location is quite fabulous—steps from Central Park and the American Museum of Natural History, with the subway practically underfoot. The building is grand, too, heavy on the wood paneling, faux-oils and gilt frames. Rooms, though not beautiful in generic brocades and stripes, are fine; even some standard rooms over-look the park.

➕ C6 ✉ 45 W 81st Street/Columbus ☎ 212/362-9200 🚇 B, C 81st Street–Museum of Natural History

FOUR SEASONS $$$

www.fourseasons.com

The grandiose I. M. Pei building makes a big first impression—all

B&BS

Those who'd like to experience the city more like a local may opt to stay in a B&B, which you'll find in all five boroughs. Often located in historic brownstones in charming neighborhoods, many offer great prices. (Be aware that some B&Bs don't actually include the second B, breakfast.) Visit www.bedandbreakfast.com/new-york-city-new-york.html for listings.

towering lobbies, marble and mez-zanine lounges. The rooms don't disappoint. In beiges and creams, they're big, with tons of closets, tubs that fill in no time and, in some, great views. Many consider this Manhattan's top hotel.

➕ E9 ✉ 57 E 57th Street, Park–Madison avenues ☎ 212/758-5700 🍴 The Garden, L'Atelier de Joël Robuchon 🚇 N, R Fifth Avenue

HOTEL 17 $

www.hotel17ny.com

The kitschy decor almost looks deliberate—its stripey wallpaper, floral bedspread, nylon carpet look seems to hit a chord with rock 'n' roll types and models. That could also be on account of its brown-stone Gramercy Park location and its dirt cheap rates. It offers shared or private baths.

➕ F15 ✉ 225 E 17th Street/2nd–3rd ave-nues ☎ 212/475-2845 🚇 L 3rd Avenue

SLEEP

THE ALGONQUIN $$

The Algonquin is forever associated with the only group of literary wits to be named after a piece of furniture: the Algonquin Round Table. The bon viveurs achieved almost as much at the bar here as they did in the pages of the embryonic *New Yorker*, with Robert Benchley, Dorothy Parker and Alexander Woolcott well ensconced. The hotel's Rose Room still contains the very table they occupied. ➕ D11 ✉ 59 West 44th Street ☎ 212/840-6800, www.algonquinhotel.com 🚇 B, D, F, M 42nd Street–Bryant Park, 7 5th Avenue

Rooftop pool at Hotel Gansevoort

HOTEL BEACON $$

www.beaconhotel.com

In the middle of Broadway, on the Upper West Side, the Beacon feels much more like an apartment building than a hotel. Some of the 200-plus rooms here have kitchenettes.

➕ B7 ✉ 2130 Broadway/75th Street ☎ 212/787-1100 🚇 1, 2, 3 72nd Street

HOTEL BELLECLAIRE $

www.hotelbelleclaire.com

Mark Twain lived here, as did Maxim Gorky. Now the early-20th-century building offers 230 clean, minimal guest rooms, with pine furniture and pale apricot-color walls, though only the rooms with shared bathrooms are budget.

➕ B6 ✉ 250 W 77th Street/Broadway ☎ 212/362-7700 🚇 1 79th Street

HOTEL GANSEVOORT $$$

www.hotelgansevoort.com

Fashion-obsessed young creatives consider this illuminated glass tower style-central. The stark guest rooms are furnished in stone and sand colors and equipped with lots of high-tech gadgets. Facilities include a rooftop pool, a spa, the Provocateur Nightclub, and the Plunge restaurant and bar.

➕ C16 ✉ 18 9th Avenue/13th Street ☎ 212/206-6700 🚇 A, C, E 14th Street; L 8th Avenue

HOTEL WOLCOTT $

www.wolcott.com

Within walking distance of Macy's, the Empire State Building and other attractions, this hotel is great value for money. It has comfortable rooms with private bath and even offers free morning coffee and muffins.

➕ D13 ✉ 4 W 31st Street, between 5th Avenue and Broadway ☎ 212/268-2900 🚇 B, D, F, M, N, Q, R 34th Street–Herald Square

THE HUDSON $$

www.hudsonhotel.com

All subdued lighting, trendy staff and minimalist chic, The Hudson is a short hop from Central Park (great for an early morning run) and a subway stop with good connections. It comes alive at night with a fashionable bar and there is

THE LIBRARY HOTEL $$

Each floor of the hotel is dedicated to a subject category from the Dewey Decimal system and each room has a collection of art and books related to a subcategory. The interior is modern and minimalist. Amenities include multiline phones with high-speed Internet access. ➕ E11 ✉ 299 Madison Avenue/41st Street ☎ 212/983-4500, www.libraryhotel.com 🚇 S, 4, 5 6 7 Grand Central–42nd Street a basement gym. Request a room (these are tiny, even by NY standards) overlooking the atrium as they tend to be quieter.

🔲 B9 ✉ 356 W 58th Street/Columbus Avenue ☎ 212/554-6000 🚇 1, A, C, B, D 59th Street–Columbus Circle

INN AT IRVING PLACE $$$

www.innatirving.com

With just 12 guest rooms and junior suites, this discreet hotel is set in two 1830s town houses near Gramercy Park, with elegant decor, period furniture, open fireplaces and a romantic atmosphere.

🔲 E15 ✉ 56 Irving Place/17th Street ☎ 212/533-4600 🚇 4, 5, 6, L, N, Q, R 14th Street–Union Square

JOLLY MADISON HOTEL $$

www.jollymadison.com

This is a very charming Italian-run boutique hotel located on Madison Avenue. It has warmth, elegance and style, but what sets it apart is a blend of 1920s American architecture and modern facilities coupled with extremely comfortable and spacious rooms.

🔲 E12 ✉ 22 E 38th Street/Madison ☎ 212/802-0600 🚇 B, D, F, M 42nd Street–Bryant Square

MANDARIN ORIENTAL $$$

www.mandarinoriental.com/newyork

This chain is known for its clean lines, its fabulous spas and excellent service. The best of the 248 rooms and suites have lovely panoramic views across Central Park or over the Hudson.

🔲 C9 ✉ 80 Columbus Circle/60th Street ☎ 212/805-8800 🍴 Asiate 🚇 A, C, B, D, 1 59th Street–Columbus Circle

MARITIME HOTEL $$

www.themaritimehotel.com

Super-hip trendsters will love this quirky 120-room place in the thick of the Meatpacking District. Porthole windows facing the Hudson and navy-blue soft furnishings add to the ship-like feel of the small rooms. It also has a fitness center, a happening bar scene and an Italian restaurant.

🔲 C15 ✉ 363 W 16th Street/9th Avenue ☎ 212/242-4300 🍴 Tao Downtown 🚇 A, C, E 14th Street

SLEEP

View over Manhattan from Rockefeller Center

MILLENNIUM BROADWAY $$

www.millenniumhotels.com

The Millennium is a good choice for theater-lovers as it's walking distance from 40 Broadway shows and several off-Broadway theaters, as well as Times Square. The high-ceilinged lobby leads to a 52-story building, with 750 guest rooms, and suites that have floor-to-ceiling windows for great views.

🚩 D11 ✉ 145 W 44th Street/Broadway ☎ 212/768-4400 🚇 1, 2, 3, 7, N, Q, R, S Times Square-42nd Street

OFF SOHO SUITES $$

www.offsoho.com

Since opening twenty years ago, this hotel's very off-SoHo location (on the Lower East Side bordering Nolita) has become all the rage. The suites are mini-studio apartments with no decorative advantages whatsoever but with full kitchens, private phones and satellite TV. The "Economy" suites share a kitchen and bathroom.

🚩 F18 ✉ 11 Rivington Street/Bowery ☎ 212/979-9815 🚇 F 2nd Avenue; J, Z Bowery

THE PLAZA $$$

www.theplazany.com/hotel

With 180 guest rooms and 102 luxury suites, overlooking either Fifth Avenue or Central Park, the Plaza is one of the most expensive hotels in the city. It was also the first hotel in the world to offer in-room iPads—how cool is that?

🚩 D9 ✉ 5th Avenue at Central Park South ☎ 212/759-3000 🚇 N, Q, R 5th Avenue–59th Street

RITZ-CARLTON BATTERY PARK $$$

www.ritzcarlton.com

This glass-sided tower has one thing no other hotel has: Views of New York Harbor. Decor is pale and contemporary, and the service and facilities are exemplary.

🚩 D23 ✉ 2 West Street/Battery Place ☎ 212/344-0800 🚇 1 South Ferry

ST. REGIS $$$

www.stregisnewyork.com

Offering Louis XV style in the middle of Midtown, this hotel has 229 extremely plush rooms and suites and gives discreet service.

St. Regis, a luxurious option in Midtown

➕ E9–E10 ✉ 2 E 55th Street/5th Avenue ☎ 212/753-4500 🚇 E, M 5th Avenue–53rd Street

THE SHOREHAM $$$

www.shorehamhotel.com

The sleek Shoreham Hotel, behind the Museum of Modern Art, has 177 small but nice rooms and suites, with suede walls, diffused lighting and soft white comforters on the beds. The choice rooms are at the back of the hotel. Extras such as Aveda products, free round-the-clock cappuccino and espresso and a hotel-curated art gallery, plus high-end technology (Bose Wave, plasma screens) in the better rooms add good value.

➕ D10 ✉ 33 W 55th Street/5th–6th avenues ☎ 212/247-6700 🚇 B, Q 57th Street

THE TIME $$

www.thetimeny.com

Just off Times Square, the 164 rooms and 28 suites sport bold, primary colors. Choose a red, yellow or blue room and you'll find that color not only covering the bed and selected wall parts but also appearing in candy and scent form. A Bose radio and Molton Brown toiletries add value but can't make the small rooms grow any larger, though you can spread out a bit in the small gym and rather swank lounge and restaurant.

➕ C11 ✉ 224 W 49th Street/between Broadway and 8th Avenue ☎ 212/246-5252 🚇 N, Q, R, S, 1, 2, 3, 7 Times Square–42nd Street

WASHINGTON SQUARE $$

www.washingtonsquarehotel.com

The only hotel in the heart of Greenwich Village has long been a favorite of musicians, writers and artists. The smart, comfortable rooms have retro-style furniture, while the beautiful lobby has a bright 1930s-style Parisian air and friendly, multilingual staff. Extras include complimentary breakfast, WiFi and gym; and there are two bars and the North Square restaurant (▷ 147).

➕ E16 ✉ 103 Waverley Place/MacDougal Street ☎ 212/777-9515 🍴 North Square restaurant 🚇 A, C, E, B, D, F, M 4th Street–Washington Square

The Shoreham's bar

SLEEP

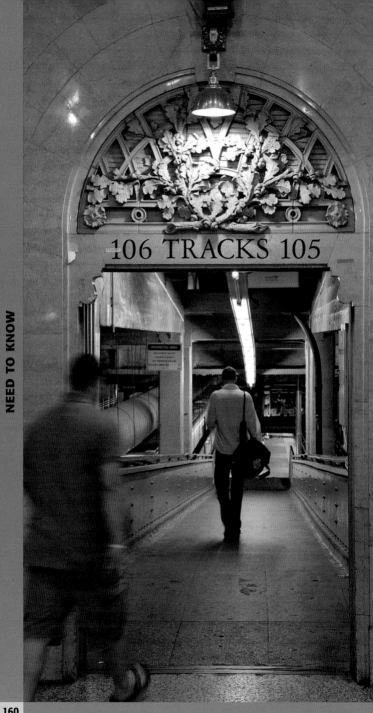

Need to Know

This section takes you through all the practical aspects of your trip to make it run more smoothly and to give you confidence before you go and while you are there.

NEED TO KNOW

Planning Ahead

WHEN TO GO

Fall is generally thought the best time to visit New York. In August many New Yorkers are driven out of town by the searing heat. However, during this time lines are shorter, restaurant reservations easier and outdoor festivals at their peak. The city has occasional blizzards in winter, but these rarely cause disruption.

TIME

New York is on Eastern Standard Time, three hours ahead of Los Angeles and five hours behind the UK.

TEMPERATURE

	JAN	FEB	MAR	APR	MAY	JUN	JUL	AUG	SEP	OCT	NOV	DEC
	39°F	41°F	46°F	61°F	70°F	81°F	84°F	82°F	77°F	66°F	54°F	39°F
	4°C	5°C	8°C	16°C	21°C	27°C	29°C	28°C	25°C	19°C	12°C	4°C

Spring (March to May) is unpredictable—even in April snow showers can alternate with shirtsleeves weather—but the worst of winter is over by mid-March.
Summer (June to August) can be extremely hot and humid, especially July and August, when the heat can make sightseeing exhausting.
Fall (September to November) sees warm temperatures persisting into October.
Winter (December to February) can be severe, with heavy snow, biting winds and subfreezing temperatures.

WHAT'S ON

January/February *Chinese New Year* (Chinatown).
February Westminster Kennel Club Dog Show (☎ 212/213-3165).
March 17 *St. Patrick's Day Parade* (5th Avenue, 44th–86th streets).
March/April *Easter Parade* (5th Avenue, 44th–57th streets).
April–October *Baseball season*
May *9th Avenue International Food Festival* (9th Avenue, 37th–57th streets ☎ 212/581-7217).
June *Metropolitan Opera park concerts* (☎ 212/362-6000).
Lesbian and Gay Pride Parade (52nd Street and 5th Avenue to Christopher and Greenwich streets).
June–September *Shakespeare in the Park* (Delacorte Theater ☎ 212/539-8750).
NY Philharmonic park concerts.
July 4 *Independence Day*
July–August *Harlem Week* (☎ 212/862-8477).
Lincoln Center Out-of-Doors Festival (☎ 212/875-5000).
August–September *US Open Tennis Championships* (☎ 718/760-6200).
September *Feast of San Gennaro* (Little Italy).
September–October *New York Film Festival* (Lincoln Center ☎ 212/875-5601).
October *Columbus Day Parade* (5th Avenue, 44th–79th streets).
November *NYC Marathon* (Staten Island to Central Park, www.nycmarathon.org).
Macy's Thanksgiving Day Parade (✉ Central Park West, 77th Street ☎ 212/494-4495).
December *Tree Lighting Ceremony* (✉ Rockefeller Center ☎ 212/332-6868).
New Year's Eve celebrations (✉ Times Square).

NEW YORK ONLINE

www.nycgo.com
The official tourism website, linked to the NYC Information Center in Midtown, includes a calendar of events, accommodations information, news updates and lots more. The helpful trip-planning section includes themed itineraries.

www.broadway.org
The Broadway League's official site, with up-to-date information on shows, theaters and the theater district in several languages.

www.newyorkcityanswers.com
Want to know what books to read before you get to the city? Which are the best tours? Tips and tricks from native New Yorkers? This aptly named site tells all.

www.nyc.gov
As the official homepage of the City of New York, the site offers links to the Office of the Mayor as well as information about community services, legal policies, city agencies, news and weather and visitor information.

www.nyc-arts.org
With a comprehensive calendar ranging for lectures about architecture to whether the circus is in town, NYC-ARTS lives up to its catchphrase as "the complete guide."

www.nymag.com
One of the most comprehensive websites covering what's on in the city, including good restaurant reviews.

www.nytimes.com
Here you'll get an inside look at New York from one of the world's most respected newspapers. The site has links to sections covering everything from world affairs to sports.

www.timessquare.com
All about Times Square and the area around, Broadway and its theaters in particular, with booking information.

TRAVEL SITES

www.fodors.com
A complete travel-planning site. You can research prices and weather, book air tickets, cars and rooms, pose questions to fellow travelers and find links to other sites.

www.iloveny.com
Official NY State site. Information about touring the city and beyond.

www.mta.info
The Metropolitan Transportation Authority updates you on service changes and disruptions, and answers questions about buses and the subway.

INTERNET ACCESS

WiFi is becoming more ubiquitous in New York all the time (in parks, cafés, libraries, and most hotels), but it's still remarkable how many places aren't equipped—or charge a fee. Check www.nycgo.com/articles/wifi-in-nyc for up-to-date information. The MTA is bringing WiFi to many subway stations; look for the logo as you enter the station. The subways themselves aren't equipped...yet.

Getting There

ARRIVING BY LAND

● Greyhound buses from across the US and Canada and commuter buses from New Jersey arrive at the Port Authority Terminal (✉ 625 8th Avenue ☎ 212/564-8484, www.greyhound.com).
● Commuter trains use Grand Central Terminal (✉ E 42nd Street/Park Avenue ☎ 212/532-4900).
● Long-distance trains arrive at Pennsylvania Station (✉ 31st Street/ 8th Avenue).

CUSTOMS

● Non-US citizens may import duty-free: 1 liter of alcohol (this is the total allowance for wine and/or spirits), 200 cigarettes or 50 cigars and $100 of gifts. (No one under 21 can import alcohol.)
● Among restricted items for import are meat, fruit, plants, seeds and certain prescription medicines without a prescription or written statement from your doctor.

SECURITY

● Always allow plenty of time for clearing security when arriving in or departing from the US.

AIRPORTS

New York has three airports—John F. Kennedy (J.F.K.) (✉ Queens, 15 miles/24km east of Manhattan ☎ 718/244-4444), Newark (✉ New Jersey, 16 miles/25km west ☎ 973/961-6000) and LaGuardia (✉ Queens, 8 miles/13km east ☎ 718/533-3400). Most international flights arrive at J.F.K. For details, visit www.panynj.gov.

LaGuardia Airport
8 miles (13km) to city center. Bus/minibus 40–45 minutes, $14

J.F.K. International Airport
15 miles (24km) to city center. Bus/minibus 1 hour, $16

Newark Liberty International Airport
16 miles (25km) to city center. Bus/minibus 40 minutes, $21

24km (15 miles) | 16km (10 miles) | 8km (5 miles) | Manhattan

ENTRY REQUIREMENTS

Visitors to New York from outside the US must have a full passport valid for the length of their stay and a return ticket. Under the Visa Waiver Program (VWP), visitors from most European countries, Australia, New Zealand, Japan and others do not need a visa to enter the US for stays of up to 90 days. For a full, current list of these countries check the US State Department website www.travel.state.gov, under "Visas."

All VWP visitors must have machine-readable passports, and all passports issued or renewed after October 26, 2006 must be e-passports containing additional biometric information. Children and infants must each have their own passport; they cannot be included on a parent's passport.

All visitors are required to obtain an electronic authorization to travel at least 72 hours prior to departure. Registration must be done under the Electronic System for Travel Authorization (ESTA™), part of the US Department of Homeland Security. (Visitors who possess a current, valid visa do not need to fill out the ESTA™ application.) Visitors who do not obtain ESTA™ clearance at least

72 hours in advance can be denied boarding or entry to the US. For more information and to fill out the application (in several languages), go to the ESTA™ website: https://esta.cbp.dhs.gov/esta/. Further information is available on: www.cbp.gov/travel/international-visitors/esta.

There is a $14 fee payable for the ESTA™ authorization for all visitors in the VWP (▷ panel, right). Payment must be made by credit or debit card when filling out the application online. The authorization is valid for two years from the date of arrival in the US.

FROM J.F.K.

The journey to Manhattan takes around an hour. NYC Airporter express bus (tel 718/777-5111) runs every 20–30 minutes, 5am–11.30pm ($16). The SuperShuttle (▷ panel, right) runs to Manhattan 24 hours a day ($19). To reserve a place, use the courtesy telephone next to the Ground Transportation Desk. Taxis cost $52 plus tolls and tip; use the official taxi stand. The AirTrain to Jamaica (E, J, Z subway and Long Island Railroad) or Howard Beach (A subway) costs $5 and takes 12 minutes, plus 35–75 minutes to Midtown. It runs every 5–10 minutes, 24 hours a day.

FROM NEWARK

It takes approximately 40 to 60 minutes to Manhattan. AirTrain (tel 888/397-4636) goes direct from all terminals 24 hours a day to Newark airport station, from which NJ Tranist operates to Penn Station in Manhattan. SuperShuttle (▷ panel, right) runs a minibus to Midtown 24 hours a day ($21). A taxi costs $50–$80, plus tolls and a $15 surcharge from Manhattan.

FROM LAGUARDIA

The journey from LaGuardia Airport to Manhattan takes between 40 and 60 minutes. SuperShuttle (▷ panel, right) runs a shared minibus 24 hours (cost $15). Services to Manhattan are also provided by NYC Airporter (cost $14; ▷ above). Taxis cost $25–$37 to Manhattan, plus tolls and tip.

Getting Around

LOST PROPERTY

● You are unlikely to recover items, but try the following (or call 311, city helpline):
Subway and bus
☎ 212/712-4500
Taxi
☎ 212/639-9675
JFK
☎ 718/244-4225/6
LaGuardia
☎ 718/533-3988
Newark
☎ 973/961-6243
Report a loss quickly if claiming on your insurance.

SUBWAY TIPS

● If your Metrocard doesn't work, don't go to a different turnstile or you'll lose a fare. As the display says, you should "swipe again."
● Check the circular signs on the outside of the cars to make sure you're boarding the correct train. Often two lines share a platform.
● Look at the boards above your head to check whether you're on the up- or downtown side and/or on the local or express track.

TAXIS

NYC–Licenced Taxis
☎ 212/639-9675
www.nyc.gov/taxi
Carmel Car and Limousine
☎ 212/666-6666
Dial 7 Car and Limousine
☎ 212/777-7777

BUSES

● Bus stops are near corners, marked by a sign and a yellow painted curb. Any ride costs the same as the subway–use a Metrocard or correct change ($2.75; $3 single ride; coins only).
● Bus maps are available from token booth clerks in subway stations.
● Buses are safe and clean but can be very slow during rush hour. The fastest are Select Buses. (For these limited stop buses, swipe your Metrocard at the fare kiosk before boarding.)
● If you pay by Metrocard you may transfer free from bus–subway or bus–bus within two hours of the time you paid the fare.

SUBWAY

● New York subway lines often close or are diverted for maintenance on weekends, especially in Lower Manhattan and Brooklyn. Check the latest information (24 hours) before you travel (tel 511 or 718/330-1234, www. mta.info). New York's subway has 24 routes and 468 stations, many open 24 hours (those with a green globe outside are always staffed).
● Visit tripplanner.mta.info for accurate point-to-point subway directions.
● To ride the subway you need a Metrocard, which you can refill. Swipe the card to enter the turnstile. Refillable Metro cards are more economical than buying single-ride tickets, and you can share the card with a companion. You can top up the card at ticket machines inside the stations for any amount. The best deal are weekly or monthly unlimited ride Metrocards, but these cannot be shared.
● Many stations have separate entrances for up- and downtown services, often on opposite corners of the street. Check the subway map and listen to the platform announcements to determine if a train is local or express and will stop at your station.
● Children under 44in (113cm) tall ride free.
● Subways run all night, with many lines (such as the 1, 2, 3, 4, 5, 6) still crowded until well after midnight. Late night riders should avoid less popular routes and always stay in the "off hour waiting area" until the train arrives.

TAXIS

● The ubiquitous yellow cab is a New York trademark and, except possibly on very wet or busy evenings, very easy to hail. Hotel concierges can arrange and most bars, restaurants and nightspots will be able to assist. If you want to book something in advance try one of the companies in the Taxis panel (left).
● Cab drivers are notorious for (a) knowing nothing about New York geography, (b) not speaking English, and (c) having an improvisational driving style.
● Tip at least 15 percent. Bills larger than $10 are unpopular for short journeys.

DRIVING

● Driving in New York is not recommended, but a car is essential for going farther afield.
● The address of the nearest major car-rental outlet can be found by calling the following toll-free numbers:
Avis, tel 800/331-1212
Budget, tel 800/527-0700
Hertz, tel 800/654-3131
National, tel 877/222-9058.
● If driving in New York is unavoidable, make sure you understand the restrictions because penalties for infringements are stringent.
● In many streets parking alternates daily from one side to the other and it is illegal to park within 10ft (3m) either side of a fire hydrant. A car illegally parked will be towed away and the driver heavily fined. Parking is expensive.
● Within the city limits the speed limit is 25mph (40kph); right turns at a red light are prohibited.
● Passing a stopped school bus is illegal and stiff fines can be imposed.

WALKING

New York is a great city for walking. If the weather is dry (if it isn't, umbrella vendors soon materialize), it's far nicer (and often faster) to hike a 10- or 20-block distance than to take the subway, or sit in a cab or bus stalled in traffic. To work it out, figure one minute per short block (north–south) and four per long block (east–west, on cross streets).

OUTER BOROUGHS

Subway lines that appear to be identical in Manhattan often diverge in other boroughs, so make certain you know which line goes to your stop. Every major subway line goes through Manhattan except the G, which serves Queens and Brooklyn exclusively.

VISITORS WITH DISABILITIES

City law requires that all facilities constructed after 1987 provide complete access to people with disabilities. Many owners of older buildings have willingly added disability-access features as well. Two important resources are the Mayor's Office for People with Disabilities (✉ 100 Gold Street, 2nd floor, 10038 ☎ 212/639-9675, www.nyc.gov/mopd) and Hospital Audiences' guide to New York's cultural institutions, *Access for All* (☎ 212/575-7676, www.hainyc.org). This online guide describes the accessibility of each place, with information on hearing and visual aids, alternative entrances and the height of telephones and water fountains. H.A. also provides descriptions of theater performances for people with visual impairments.

Essential Facts

VISITOR INFORMATION

The city runs visitor information centers and kiosks around town. The most comprehensive is at Macy's (▷ 123) ✉ Herald Square ☎ 212/484-1222, www.nycgo.com
🕐 Mon–Fri 9–7, Sat 10–7, Sun 11–7
Touch screens allow visitors to research attractions and the center offers discount coupons, including to Macy's.

EMERGENCY NUMBERS

● Police, Fire Department, Ambulance ☎ 911
● Crime Victims Hotline ☎ 212/577-7777
● Sex Crimes Report Line ☎ 212/267-7273

ELECTRICITY

● The supply is 120 volts, 60 hz AC current.
● US appliances use flat two-prong plugs. European appliances require an adapter and a voltage transformer.

ETIQUETTE

● Tipping: waitstaff get 15–20 percent (roughly double the 8.875 percent sales tax); so do cab drivers. Bartenders get about the same (though less than $1 is stingy). Bellhops ($1 per bag), room service waiters (10 percent) and hairdressers (15–20 percent) should also be tipped.
● There are stringent smoking laws in New York. Smoking is banned on public transportation, in cabs, in all places of work, including restaurants and bars, and, since 2011, in all city parks, on beaches and in Times Square.

MAIL AND TELEPHONES

● The main post office (8th Avenue/33rd Street, tel 212/330-3296) is open daily. Visit www.usps.com to find neighborhood branches.
● Stamps are also available from hotel concierges, online at www.usps.com, at some delis and from vending machines in stores.
● All New York numbers require the area code (212, 718, 646, 347 or 917) when dialing. For long-distance calls, add 1 before the code.
● Hotels often levy surcharges for making calls.
● Foreign visitors: Watch out for mobile roaming charges that can result in a large bill on your return home; it's best to ask your mobile provider for information on data plans that can be used in the United States.
● To call the US from the UK, dial 001. To call the UK from the US, dial 011 44, then drop the first zero from the area code.

MEDICAL TREATMENT

● It is essential to have adequate insurance.
● In the event of an emergency, the 911 operator will send an ambulance.
● Doctors on Call (24 hours), tel 212/737-1212.

- Near Midtown, 24-hour emergency rooms: Mt. Sinai Roosevelt Hospital, 10th Avenue and 59th Street, tel 212/523-4000.
- Dental Emergency Service, tel 646/837-7806. An operator will put you in touch with a dentist close to you open 24/7.

MONEY MATTERS
- Credit cards are widely accepted. Visa, MasterCard, American Express, Diner's Card and Discover are the ones that are most commonly used.
- US dollar traveler's checks are hard to use outside hotels and currency exchange offices. It is difficult to exchange foreign currency travelers' checks, even at banks, and fees are high.

NEWSPAPERS AND MAGAZINES
- The local papers are the *New York Times* (with a Sunday edition), the *Daily News* (also with Sunday supplements) and the *New York Post*. The free alternative paper the *Village Voice* includes extensive listings. The *Wall Street Journal*, once soley a financial daily, now covers the arts scene in New York on par with the *New York Times*.
- Pick up *Time Out New York*, the *New Yorker*, and *New York* magazine on newsstands; the glossier *In New York* and *Where* can be found in hotels and both showcase events.
- Monday to Friday, the free dailies *amNY* and *Metro New York* are handed out at virtually every Manhattan subway station and feature news and event listings.

OPENING HOURS
- Banks: Mon–Fri 9–3 or 3.30; some are open longer, and on Saturday.
- Stores: Mon–Sat 10–6; many are open far later, and on Sunday 12–6; those in the Village, Nolita and SoHo open and close later.
- Museums: hours vary, but Monday is the most common closing day.
- Post offices: Mon–Fri 8 or 9–6. Some open Sat 9–4.
- Opening times given are for general guidance only.

MONEY
The unit of currency is the dollar (= 100 cents). Bills (notes) come in denominations of $1, $2, $5, $10, $20, $50 and $100; coins come in 25¢ (a quarter), 10¢ (a dime), 5¢ (a nickel) and 1¢ (a penny).
Note: American coins are not marked with numerals (e.g. the 25 cent piece says "quarter dollar" only).

TRAVEL INSURANCE
A minimum of $1 million medical cover is advised. Choose a policy that covers baggage and document loss, and cancellation.

PUBLIC HOLIDAYS
- New Year's Day: January 1
- Martin Luther King, Jr. Day: third Monday of January
- Presidents' Day: third Monday of February
- Memorial Day: last Monday in May
- Independence Day: July 4
- Labor Day: first Monday in September
- Columbus Day: second Monday in October
- Veterans' Day: November 11
- Thanksgiving Day: fourth Thursday of November
- Christmas Day: December 25

NEED TO KNOW

CONSULATES

Australia
✉ 150 E 42nd Street
☎ 212/351-6500
Canada
✉ 1251 6th Avenue
☎ 212/596-1628
Denmark
✉ 885 2nd Avenue,
18th Floor
☎ 212/223-4545
France
✉ 934 5th Avenue
☎ 212/606-3600
Germany
✉ 871 UN Plaza
☎ 212/610-9700
Ireland
✉ 345 Park Avenue
☎ 212/319-2555
Italy
✉ 690 Park Avenue
☎ 212/737-9100
Norway
✉ 825 3rd Avenue
☎ 646/430-7500
Spain
✉ 150 East 58th Street,
30th Floor
☎ 212/355/4080
UK
✉ 845 3rd Avenue
☎ 212/745-0200

REST ROOMS

● Almost every department store has facilities, as do many smaller stores and key visitor attractions. Hotel lobbies, restaurants and bars offer rest rooms. Exercise caution when using facilities at public transportation hubs or in less salubrious neighborhoods.

RADIO AND TELEVISION

● NY1 is the main cable channel serving the New York boroughs and will give you access to news, weather and travel as well as its own take on daily life in the Big Apple.
● WNYC (New York Public Radio) on 93.9 FM and 820 AM has news, culture and music items.
● Many TV shows are filmed in New York, from *Good Morning America* to the *Daily Show*. Go to www.nycgo.com/tv-show-tapings for further details.

SENSIBLE PRECAUTIONS

● Maintain awareness of your surroundings and of other people, and try to look as though you know your way around.
● Avoid the quieter subway lines at night and also certain areas of Brooklyn. Areas of Manhattan once considered unsafe (Alphabet City east of Avenue C, the far west of Midtown, north of about 110th Street and Central Park) are less edgy than they used to be. Still, keep your wits about you in deserted areas.
● Conceal your wallet; keep the fastener of your bag on the inside; and don't flash large amounts of cash or jewelry.

STUDENTS

● An International Student Identity Card (ISIC) is good for reduced admission at many museums, theaters and other attractions.
● Carry the ISIC or some other photo ID card to prove you're a fulltime student or over 21.
● Under-25s will find it expensive to rent a car.

VISITOR PASSES

Two visitor passes offer big savings if you're planning to take in multiple attractions: New York CityPass ($114 adults, $89 children, www.citypass.com) is valid for nine days and covers six top attractions, including the Statue of Liberty, Empire State Building and major museums. If you opt for the Explorer Pass (from $79.99 adults, $61.99 children, www.smartdestinations.com), you can choose 3, 5, 7, or 10 attractions from a list of 50 top sights and tours; valid for 30 days.

Books and Films

BOOKS
Non-fiction

- *The Historical Atlas of New York City* by Eric Homberger (1998), Henry Holt and Company.
- *Here is New York* by E.B. White (2000), Little Bookroom.
- *Inside the Apple: A Streetwise History of New York City* by Michelle and James Nevius (2009), Free Press.
- *The New York Nobody Knows: Walking 6,000 Miles in the City* (2013), Princeton University Press.
- *The New York Times' Book of New York* (2009), Black Dog & Leventhal Publishers.
- *Five Points* by Tyler Anbinder (2001), Free Press.

MOVIES

42nd Street (1933), Lloyd Bacon
King Kong (1933), Merian C. Cooper
Guys and Dolls (1955), Joseph L. Mankiewicz
Breakfast at Tiffany's (1961), Blake Edwards
West Side Story (1961), Robert Wise
The French Connection (1971), William Friedkin
Mean Streets (1973), Martin Scorsese
Taxi Driver (1976), Martin Scorsese
Saturday Night Fever (1977), John Badham
Manhattan (1979), Woody Allen
Broadway Danny Rose (1984), Woody Allen
The Cotton Club (1984), Francis Ford Coppola
Desperately Seeking Susan (1985), Susan Seidelman
Radio Days (1987), Woody Allen
Do the Right Thing (1989), Spike Lee
When Harry Met Sally (1989), Rob Reiner
A Bronx Tale (1993), Robert De Niro
Pollock (2000), Ed Harris
Requiem for a Dream (2000), Darren Aronofsky
Gangs of New York (2002), Martin Scorsese
The Devil Wears Prada (2006), David Franke
Night at the Museum (2006), Shawn Levy
Julie and Julia (2009), Nora Ephron
The Adjustment Bureau (2011) J. J. Abrams
Inside Llewyn Davis (2013), Joel and Ethan Coen
Birdman: Or (The Unexpected Virtue of Ignorance) (2014), Alejandro González Iñárritu

FICTION

F. Scott Fitzgerald's *The Beautiful and Damned* (1922), John Dos Passos's *Manhattan Transfer* (1925), J. D. Salinger's *The Catcher in the Rye* (1951) and Truman Capote's *Breakfast at Tiffany's* (1958) are all classic reads. Also recommended are Tom Wolfe's *Bonfire of the Vanities* (1987), *The New York Trilogy* (1988) by Paul Auster, and *New York: The Novel* (2010) by Edward Rutherfurd.

Index

The Automobile Association would like to thank the following photographers, companies and picture libraries for their assistance in the preparation of this book.

2(i-v) AA J Tims; 3(i-ii) AA/J Tims; 3(iii) Gansevoort Meatpacking NYC Gansevoort Meatpacking NYC; 3(iv) AA/J Tims; 4 AA/D Pollack; 5 AA/J Tims; 6t Nick Wood/Alamy; 6b, 6/7t, 6/7c AA/J Tims; 6/7b Photolibrary; 7t Photolibrary; 7tc AA/J Tims; 8t AA/C Sawyer; 8b Pablo Valentini/Alamy; 8/9t The Dinex Group Café Boulud NYC by B. Milne; 8/9b, 9t AA/J Tims; 9tc AA/C Sawyer; 9bc NYC images/Alamy; 9b AA/J Tims; 10l AA; 10r Mary Evans Picture Library/Classic Stock/H. Armstrong Roberts; 11l Mary Evans Picture Library; 11r Lower East Side Tenement Museum Courtesy the Lower East Side Tenement Museum, photography by Keiko Niwa; 12–14/5, 15, 16 AA/J Tims, 16/7t Michael Matthews /Alamy; 16–20 AA/J Tims; 21t AA/J Tims; 21bl AA/C Sawyer; 21br AA/J Tims; 22 Sandra Baker/Alamy; 23 AA/J Tims; 24 Tetra Images /Alamy; 24/5t AA/C Sawyer; 24/5b AA/ Simon McBride; 25t The Ukrainian Museum Courtesy of The Ukrainian Museum; 25b AA/C Sawyer; 26–29 AA/J Tims; 30b Patrick Batchelder/Alamy; 30t, 30/31, 31 AA/J Tims; 32/33 The Frick Collection, New York The Frick Collection, New York Photo: Michael Bodycomb 33 The Frick Collection, New York. The Frick Collection, New York Photo: Galen Lee. 34–37 AA/J Tims; 38/39 Christian Kober/Robert Harding; 39 AA/J Tims; 40 Douglas Lander /Alamy; 40/41 Chris A Selby/Alamy; 42/43 Lincoln Center Media Desk Photo Gallery. Photo credit: Mark Bussell Lincoln Center for the Performing Arts; 43t Lincoln Center Media Desk Photo Gallery. Photo credit: Stefan Cohen Lincoln Center for the Performing Arts; 43bl Lincoln Center Media Desk Photo Gallery. Photo credit: Stefan Cohen Lincoln Center for the Performing Arts; 43br Lincoln Center Media Desk Photo Gallery. Photo credit: Mark Bussell Lincoln Center for the Performing Arts; 44/45 AA/J Tims; 45tr AA/J Tims; 45br AA/J Tims; 46 AA/J Tims, Chagall®/© ADAGP, Paris and DACS, London 2011 AND © ADAGP, Paris and DACS, London 2011. 46/7 AA/J Tims; 48tl AA/J Tims; 46bl Michal Besser /Alamy; 48–55 AA/J Tims; 56t, b AA/J Tims; 56/7b Steven Widoff /Alamy; 57tl, 57r AA/J Tims; 58–59 AA/J Tims; 60/61 The Bridgeman Art Library Dempsey and Firpo, Whitney Museum of American Art/Bridgeman; 61 Whitney Museum © Whitney Museum/Ed Lederman; 62l John Kellerman/Alamy; 62/63t Christopher Penler/Alamy; 62/63b David Cooper / Alamy; 63r Lenz/Alamy; 64 AA/J Tims; 66l American Folk Art Museum American Folk Art Museum; 66r AA/C Sawyer; 67 AA/J Tims; 68 Photolibrary; 69–71 AA/J Tims; 71r Stephen Finn/Alamy; 72 Getty Images Tetra Images/Getty Images; 73–74 AA/J Tims; 75 Photolibrary; 76 AA/J Tims; 78t AA/J Tims; 78b AA/J Tims; 79t AA/J Tims; 79b Spencer Grant /Alamy; 82(i-vi) AA/J Tims; 82(vii) John Kellerman /Alamy; 84t AA/J Tims; 84b AA/World Travel Library/Alamy; 85t AA/J Tims; 85b Aurora Photos /Alamy; 88(i, ii) AA/J Tims; 88(iii) Asia Photopress/Alamy; 88(iv) Robert Nickelsberg/Alamy; 90t AA/J Tims; 90b AA/Simon McBride; 91 AA/J Tims; 94 AA/J Tims; 96t AA/J Tims; 96b AA/J Tims; 97t AA/J Tims; 100(i) AA/J Tims; 100(ii) AA/C Sawyer; 100(iii) The Frick Collection, New York The Frick Collection, New York Photo: Michael Bodycomb; 100 AA/J Tims; 102t American Folk Art Museum American Folk Art Museum; 102b AA/J Tims; 103t Matthiola /Alamy; 103c AA/J Tims; 103b Lincoln Center Media Desk Photo Gallery. Photo credit: Mark Bussell Lincoln Center for the Performing Arts; 106 AA/J Tims; 107 AA/Simon McBride; 108t Prisma Bildagentur AG/Alamy; 108b AA/J Tims; 109t Alamy Richard Ellis/Alamy; 109b AA/J Tims; 112, 113, 114 AA/J Tims; 116/117t AA/J Tims; 116/117mt, mb AA/J Tims; 116/117b Richard Levine /Alamy; 117mt AA/J Tims; 117mb AA/C Sawyer; 119, 120, 123 AA/J Tims; 124 Yadid Levy/Alamy; 126 AA/J Tims; 128 Prisma Bildagentur AG/Alamy; 128/9t Jon Arnold Images Ltd /Alamy; 128/9tc AA/J Tims; 128/9bc Lincoln Center Media Desk Photo Gallery. Photo credit: Iwan BAA/n Lincoln Center for the Performing Arts; 128, 129, 131, 132 AA/J Tims; 136 AA/Paul Kenward; 138 AA/J Tims; 140t AA/J Tims; 140tc AA/C Sawyer; 140bc The Dinex Group Café Boulud NYC by B. Milne; 141 AA/J Tims; 143 AA/J Tims; 145 AA/Julian Love; 146 Kathy deWitt/Alamy; 150 Gansevoort Meatpacking NYC; 150 Gansevoort Meatpacking NYC; 152t Gansevoort Meatpacking NYC Gansevoort Meatpacking NYC 152tc Shoreham hotel; 152bc CROSBY STREET/www.crosbystreethotel.com; 152b Shoreham hotel; 154l CROSBY STREET HOTEL/www.crosbystreethotel.com; 154r Four Seasons Hotels and Resorts/Saylor, Durston Four Seasons Hotels and Resorts; 156 Gansevoort Meatpacking NYC Gansevoort Meatpacking NYC; 157 AA/J Tims; 158 AA/C Sawyer; 159 Shoreham hotel; 160 AA/J Tims.

Every effort has been made to trace the copyright holders, and we apologise in advance for any unintentional omissions or errors. We would be pleased to apply any corrections in a following edition of this publication.

New York City 25 Best

WRITTEN BY Kate Sekules
ADDITIONAL WRITING BY Donna Dailey
UPDATED BY James and Michelle Nevius
SERIES EDITOR Clare Ashton
COVER DESIGN Chie Ushio, Yuko Inagaki
DESIGN WORK Tracey Freestone
IMAGE RETOUCHING AND REPRO Jacqueline Street-Elkayam

Published in the United Kingdom by AA Publishing

ISBN 978-1-1018-7947-4

TWELFTH EDITION

All details in this book are based on information supplied to us at press time. Always confirm information when it matters, especially if you're making a detour to visit a specific place. Fodor's expressly disclaims any liability, loss, or risk, personal or otherwise, that is incurred as a consequence of the use of any of the contents of this book.

SPECIAL SALES
This book is available for special discounts for bulk purchases for sales promotions or premiums. For more information, email specialmarkets@randomhouse.com.

Color separation by AA Digital Department
Printed and bound by Leo Paper Products, China

10 9 8 7 6 5 4 3 2 1

A05314
Maps in this title produced from mapping data supplied by Global Mapping, Brackley, UK © Global Mapping and data from openstreetmap.org
© OpenStreetMap contributors
Transport map © Communicarta Ltd, UK

Titles in the Series